IMAGES
of America

Tualatin Valley Fire & Rescue

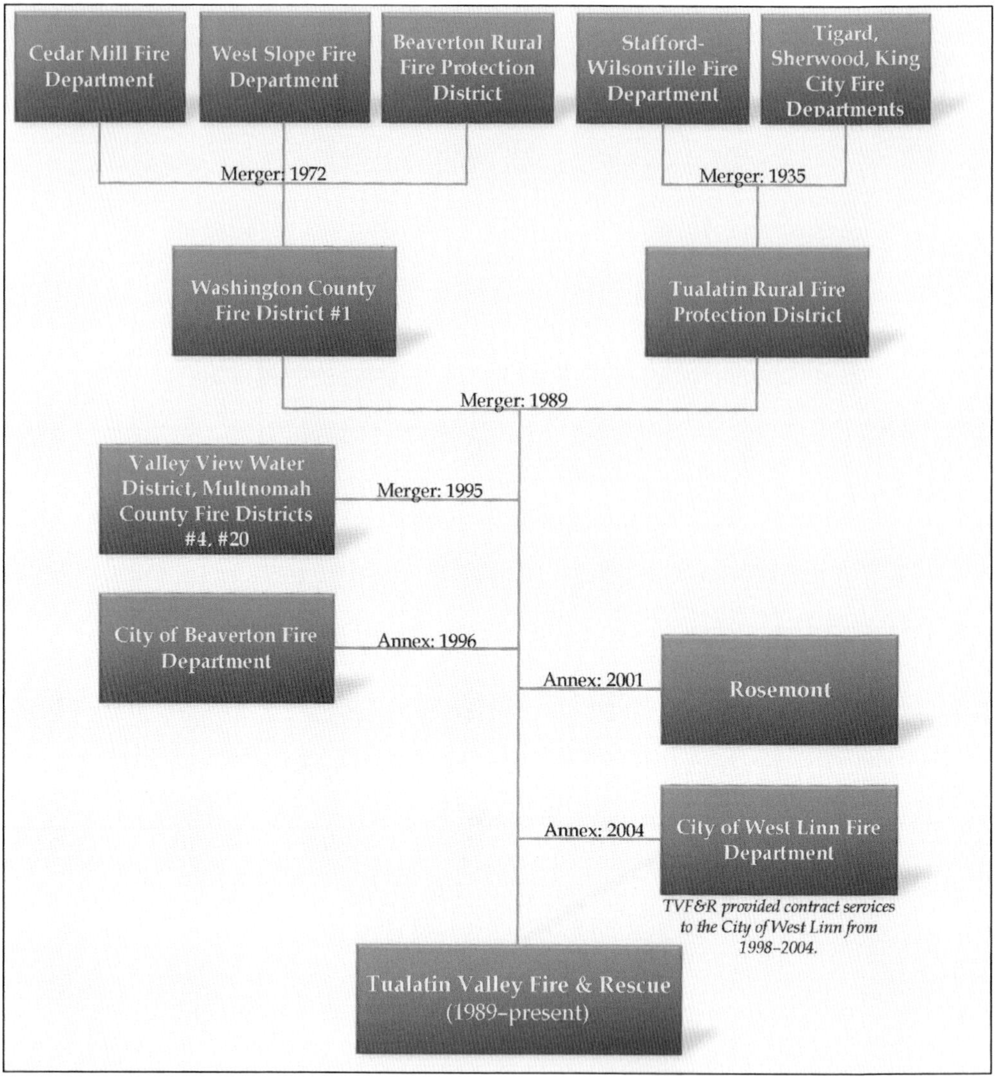

The merger of many fire departments over the years—including the Beaverton Fire Department, Tualatin Rural Fire Protection District, and Washington County Fire District No. 1—created the expansive and nationally recognized Tualatin Valley Fire & Rescue. Here is a timeline of when each department joined the fire district. (Tualatin Valley Fire & Rescue.)

On the Cover: Members of Tualatin Rural Fire Protection District stand in front of the department's first-aid car around 1955. They are, from left to right, Floyd Berning, Marion "Dutch" Maxwell, Chief William Barngrover, and Assistant Chief Dell Heald. Both Barngrover and firefighter Merwyn Conover personally went out to Texas to retrieve the vehicle when it was originally purchased. (Rita Barngrover Conover collection, courtesy of Tualatin Historical Society.)

IMAGES
of America

TUALATIN VALLEY FIRE & RESCUE

Ray Pitz

ARCADIA
PUBLISHING

ISBN 978-0-7385-9304-3

Published by Arcadia Publishing
Charleston, South Carolina

Printed in the United States of America

Library of Congress Control Number: 2011937147

For all general information, please contact Arcadia Publishing:
Telephone 843-853-2070
Fax 843-853-0044
E-mail sales@arcadiapublishing.com
For customer service and orders:
Toll-Free 1-888-313-2665

Visit us on the Internet at www.arcadiapublishing.com

To my wife, Irene, for all her love and support, and to my father, Walter, for giving me a curiosity about history and how things work

Contents

Foreword

It is not often that a fire department has a lineage that includes 14 departments. However, that can be said of Tualatin Valley Fire & Rescue (TVF&R). Our fire department took shape between 1935 and 1989, as nine fire departments located throughout Washington, Clackamas, and Multnomah counties consolidated to increase efficiency, lower the cost of services, and eliminate duplication. From 1995 through 2004, five more fire departments chose to join Tualatin Valley Fire & Rescue, making it Oregon's largest fire district. Each of our predecessor departments had rich histories, traditions, and cultures that have helped shape Tualatin Valley Fire & Rescue. Despite evolving into a sophisticated organization that responds to over 30,000 incidents each year, we strive to be the "hometown" fire department in the communities served by our 21 stations. We do not take for granted the commitment put forth by those who came before us, and we continue to carry the mantle of stewardship and craftsmanship with pride.

—TVF&R fire chief Michael R. Duyck
September 2011

ACKNOWLEDGMENTS

This book would not have been possible without the help of some very special people.

At Arcadia, I would like to thank my editors, Shayne Ross and Donna Libert, whose help and encouragement made for a pleasant process.

Special thanks to Ernie Metcalfe and Lee Coleman—Ernie with the old Beaverton Fire Department and Lee with the old West Slope Fire Protection District and Washington County Fire District No. 1—whose vast knowledge of the old departments gave me an insightful look at the way things used to be and how they worked.

Former Tualatin Valley Fire & Rescue chiefs Jeff Johnson and Jack Snook were a wealth of information, as was current chief Mike Duyck. Oscar "Sox" Lee, former Beaverton Fire Department chief, was a help as well. Thanks to Capt. Leonard Damian and Lt. Gary Lamb for allowing me access to the scrapbook at West Slope Station 65.

Karen Eubanks and Cassandra Ulven of TVF&R were extremely helpful in locating and gaining access to photographs and finding historical information. Also, a big thanks goes out to TVF &R's Shirlee O'Connor, who helped me contact retired firefighters and was extremely enthusiastic about the project from the start.

Yvonne Addington, of the Tualatin Historical Society, was generous with providing information and in loaning me the photographs of the old Tualatin Rural Fire Protection District, as was Rita Barngrover Conover. Gary Toll's photographs from the old Tualatin Rural Fire Protection District were a great help as well. Retired firefighter Mark Kreutzer was helpful in sharing the archival negatives of photographer Harvey Thomas, and Thomas was extremely generous in allowing me use of the photographs he shot of Washington County Fire District No. 1 firefighters in the 1970s and 1980s when he was the district's official photographer.

Thanks goes out to Jessie Kirk, Mikel Kelly, Jaime Valdez, Geoff Pursinger, Steve Clark, Mark Garber, Christina Lent, and Vern Uyetake, all of Community Newspapers, for their editing and photography skills, and overall support.

Also, thanks to Virginia Bruce, Frank Oulman, Steve May, Bob Fryer, Clyde List, June Reynolds, and Odge Gribble, Don Anderson, Mary Hill, Joe Martin, Duane Watt, Jeffrey Butts, Rick Eiden, Nancy Bruton, Capt. Troy Spisla, Walt Platt, Gordon Scott, Phil Lapp, Cornelia Becker Seigneur (author of Arcadia's *West Linn*), Bev Ecker (of the Beaverton Historical Society), and Winnifred Herrschaft (of the Washington County Historical Society).

Finally, a very special thanks to Kurt Koudelka whose access to the photographs he used for the 2002 in-house book *Tualatin Valley Fire & Rescue* (which he wrote and produced along with Lynn Bruton and Scott Sullivan) set the benchmark for any definitive book on the fire district.

Throughout this book, Tualatin Valley Fire & Rescue is credited in photographs as TVF&R.

INTRODUCTION

The story of Tualatin Valley Fire & Rescue is a relatively recent one, founded when two departments merged and a third annexed into the sprawling district over the last two decades.

The impetus for coming together began in 1986 when two men, Washington County Fire District No. 1 chief Jack Snook and Tualatin Rural Fire Protection District chief Floyd Pittard, began talking about a possible consolidation between their two departments. Eliminating service duplication and reducing operating costs were among the topics of discussion.

"We started meeting every Monday from 8 a.m. to noon," recalled Snook. "After a few meetings, we said, 'should we have Beaverton involved?' "

Beaverton Fire Department chief Oscar "Sox" Lee joined the group a short time later. Over the course of the discussions, a few snags were hit; among them was the question of who should be chief. The meetings would later resume with Chief Lee suggesting that the group ultimately should consider what is in the best interests of the residents.

In 1989, Tualatin Rural Fire Protection District and Washington County District No. 1 merged to create Tualatin Valley Fire & Rescue. Jack Snook was named chief. Meanwhile, the agency worked cooperatively with Beaverton before voters of that city officially agreed to an annexation into the district in 1996.

While that is the modern story, each of the three fire departments or districts has a distinct, separate history. The oldest of those departments is Beaverton, whose first known existence is mentioned in a newspaper article from 1914.

The 1930s brought a flutter of activity for the Beaverton Volunteer Fire Department, and the city purchased a chassis for a new fire truck for $635 from a local Chevrolet dealer in 1935.

Meanwhile, Beaverton's neighbor to the south was forming its own district. Established on February 2, 1935, the Tualatin Fire Department would become the Tualatin Rural Fire Protection District in 1946. That same year, the district built its first station on Boone's Ferry Road. The Stafford-Wilsonville Fire Department and the Tigard, Sherwood, and King City Fire Departments would eventually merge with that district.

The beginning of the 1940s resulted in smaller districts sprouting up all around Beaverton.

In 1941, residents of West Slope, a community east of Beaverton, voted to allow the West Slope Water District to enter into an agreement with Beaverton to provide fire protection services. The agreement continued until West Slope Rural Fire Protection District became an independent entity in 1949 with the district's first fire truck arriving the next year.

Also in the 1940s, residents in Cedar Mill, another neighboring community, were busy thinking about fire protection as well. The Cedar Mill Rural Fire Protection District began as a fire patrol guarding against possible World War II enemy attacks before expanding into an official district in 1946. The operation was undertaken by George Foege and Dave Ediger, who were co-owners of the local Cedar Mill Garage. Foege, a gentleman who was described as having a tremendous positive influence on his young firefighters, became chief.

Not to be outdone in providing fire protection to its residents, the unincorporated community of Aloha established the Beaverton Rural Fire Protection District in 1947 with firefighters responding to calls from a station located across the street from the present Aloha Post Office on 185th Avenue. The rural district signed a contract with the City of Beaverton to provide services.

Washington County Fire District No. 1 had its beginnings in the Beaverton Rural Fire Protection District. In addition to its Aloha station, the rural district would open a second station in Progress in 1965 (equipping it with two engines), and a third station on Southwest Jenkins Road became operational in 1967, locating on property near Tektronix.

In 1972, all three of the smaller fire entities—Cedar Mill, West Slope, and Beaverton Rural—agreed to come together under the merged umbrella of Washington County Fire District No. 1.

Other mergers into TVF&R would include Valley View Water District along with Multnomah Fire Districts No. 4 and No. 20, who all merged in 1995.

While West Linn (located in neighboring Clackamas County) once had its own fire department, it began contracting for services with TVF&R in 1998—an agreement that would last until 2004 when that city would officially merge with the district. West Linn's Rosemont Fire District also would join TVF&R in 2001. Across the Willamette River from West Linn, Oregon City also would join TVF&R on a contract basis from 1999 to 2003.

With all the mergers in place, TVF&R would become the second largest fire department in Oregon, covering 216 square miles, which includes nine cities and portions of three counties. In 2010, the district boasted 319 career firefighters/EMTs and paramedics along with 76 volunteers. Today, TVF&R is a full-service department that includes specialty departments, such as a hazardous materials team, a technical rescue team, and a water rescue team.

Still, the district's modern history can be traced to the dedication and perseverance of all those who worked in the early departments to create one of the most respected fire district's in the nation.

One

Beaverton Fire Department

While the exact year the Beaverton Fire Department was established is up for debate, an iconic July 4, 1900, photograph shows so-called fire boys on parade, featuring a drum-and-fife group marching down a Beaverton street.

Over the years, there would be a debate over whether the group was actually a formal organization. Nevertheless, the first reference to the Beaverton Fire Department would come in the 1914 edition of the *Owl* newspaper, which said the department was made up of the early settlers of the area with Fred Pappel appointed as fire chief.

In 1919, a used hose cart consisting of 500 feet of two-and-a-half-inch hose was purchased along with a chemical cart containing two 15-gallon tanks. While the carts were no doubt a big help in fire suppression, their storage facility was less impressive—an old chicken shed in the Broadway Street/West Avenue area in downtown Beaverton.

In 1929, a Stutz vehicle was purchased by Beaverton and converted into a fire engine, but it was not until 1934 that the Beaverton City Council decided to pay its chief and other volunteers. It was agreed upon that the chief would make $3 a month and volunteers would get 50¢ per fire (an amount that was to include participation in one drill each month).

Archie Olson became chief in 1937, the same year that the city would move into a new city hall and fire station located at First Avenue and Angel Street. During this time, discussion of forming a rural fire district loomed large, and a 1928 Graham school bus chassis was soon purchased and retrofitted with a 600-gallon water tank. Put into service in 1939, it responded to calls in Aloha, Huber, Hazeldale, Cedar Mill, Metzger, Garden Home, and West Slope. But it would not be until 1946 that the first board of directors of the Beaverton Rural Fire Protection District signed a one-year contract with the city to provide services.

Meanwhile, having outgrown its First Avenue and Angel Street location, the Beaverton Fire Department moved into new quarters in Beaverton City Hall at Fifth Street and Hall Boulevard in June 1958. The new fire station would serve the department until the structure was torn down in the summer of 1999.

Hueston Reynolds would become chief of the Beaverton Fire Department in 1963, a position he would hold until he retired in 1985 and was succeeded by Oscar "Sox" Lee. Chief Lee retired in 1992, and Gary Nees took over until the official merger with TVF&R in 1996.

Clarence Buffam drives the Beaverton Fire Department's Engine No. 4, a 1942 Howard-Cooper Chevrolet with a 500-gallons-per-minute pump. Buffam's day job was working at the Beaverton Post Office. When a fire broke out, Buffam would gather other post office volunteer firefighters and respond to the incident. On the back of the engine is Frank Zimbrick, who worked as a Beaverton-area plumber. (Courtesy of TVF&R.)

A volunteer firefighter from the Beaverton Rural Fire Protection District mans the district's two engines, both 1946 Dodges. The equipment was kept in the downtown Beaverton Fire Department station, located then at Angel and Main Streets. During this time, the district contracted with the city to house, maintain, and operate its equipment. (Photograph by Ernie Metcalfe.)

Don Rodgers (left), Fay Evans (center), and Don Jenkins, all volunteers for the Beaverton Rural Fire Protection District, head down Tualatin Valley Highway at 170th Avenue at 2:00 p.m. on August 2, 1952, to put out a grass fire north of Aloha. Rodgers ran a Beaverton restaurant, Evans started Beaverton's first garbage service, and Jenkins was Beaverton's postmaster. Evans's headgear is a World War II civil defense helmet. (Photograph by Ernie Metcalfe.)

Members of the Beaverton Rural Fire Protection District and the Cedar Mill Fire Department mop up a fire on Merlo Road in the late 1940s or early 1950s. The two departments had mutual aid agreements. The man in the hat facing the photographer is volunteer John Barnes. (Photograph by Ernie Metcalfe.)

Above, firefighter Clarence Buffam (on rig), and Beaverton fire chief Archie Olson use a Beaverton Rural Fire Protection District engine to fight a brush fire on King Street in the Garden Home area in what is now on the Oleson Road side of the Portland Golf Club. Retired firefighter Ernie Metcalfe described Olson, who was named chief of the Beaverton Fire Department in February 1937, as "old school" when it came to firefighting. That meant telling his firefighters to "put the wet stuff on the red stuff." Below, local boys do their part in extinguishing the same fire on King Street. The fire was contained by firefighters from the Beaverton Rural Fire Protection District. (Both photographs by Ernie Metcalfe.)

A Beaverton Rural Fire Protection District crew mops up a fire at a grocery store in Garden Home in April 1953 or 1954, as a sheriff's deputy (back to camera) surveys the damage. The store was located on the corner of Oleson and Garden Home Roads now occupied by a Dairy Queen. (Photograph by Ernie Metcalfe.)

A 1953 International tanker from the Beaverton Rural Fire Protection District (foreground) helps extinguish a major fire that burned the same grocery store on the corner of Oleson and Garden Home Roads in Garden Home. Aiding in the effort was the Portland Fire Bureau, their two engines visible to the right. (Photograph by Ernie Metcalfe.)

Beaverton volunteer firefighters Walt Unis (left) and George Kline attend a fire training event at the Portland Fire Bureau's main station along with one of the fire district's 1953 International engines (in back with door open). When not fighting fires, Unis was busy running his business Beaverton Electric. Also attending the event were employees of Tualatin Rural Fire Protection District, who brought one of their engines (front). (Photograph by Ernie Metcalfe.)

Beaverton fire chief Archie Olson shows off a message placed aboard the department's 1935 Chevrolet engine in September 1960. The sign was part of a push to purchase new Pirsch engines. When Olson later retired, new chief Bob Wickam transformed the vehicle into a salvage rig where air packs and mop-up equipment were stored. (Photograph by Ernie Metcalfe.)

More than a big water fight, Indiana waterball competitions were long the sources of pride for fire departments, including Beaverton. The goal was to be the first to move a ball tethered to a guy-wire toward the opponent. Here, nozzleman Joe Thomas (second from left) and Doug Gamwell (left) battle against unknown opponents from the West Slope Fire Department (right) at a competition in Banks in July 1961. (Photograph by Ernie Metcalfe.)

Beaverton Fire Department members receive a trophy following an Indiana waterball competition victory in Banks in July 1961. They include, from left to right, (first row) John Ryan, Doug Gamwell, Bob Lambert, and Ernie Metcalfe; (second row) Doyle Harris, Joe Thomas, Jim St. Claire, and Chief Bob Wickam. The early turnouts these firefighters are wearing are nothing more than a canvas covering with a rubber liner; they were not fireproof. (Courtesy of Ernie Metcalfe.)

Victorious after a waterball competition held at Beaverton High School in August 1961, city officials and Beaverton Fire Department personnel share congratulations. Pictured are, from left to right, Mayor Bruce Nichols, Capt. Jim St. Claire, Tom Shriver (who would become chief of the West Slope Rural Fire Protection District in 1963), Joe Thomas, and unidentified. In the background leaning against the window are Chet Robinson (left) and Alden Oleson (center), Beaverton Rural Fire Protection District board members. (Photograph by Ernie Metcalfe.)

Beaverton fire chief Bob Wickam stands in front of the chief's vehicle, a 1961 International Travelall, in December 1961. Wickam was appointed chief by the Beaverton City Council in September 1960. By this time, the fire department had moved into new quarters adjacent to Beaverton City Hall at Fifth Street and Hall Boulevard. (Photograph by Ernie Metcalfe.)

This 1961 International Travelall was the chief's car. It was later turned into the Beaverton Fire Department's first first-aid vehicle. The station and accompanying city hall were torn down in 1999 to make room for the new Beaverton Public Library. In the background is the old rectory for St. Cecilia Catholic Church. (Photograph by Ernie Metcalfe.)

Here, two red, 1962 Pirsch custom pumpers arrive in Beaverton. The identical vehicles both had 1,000-gallons-per-minute, two-stage, mid-ship pumps. They could hold 500 gallons of water each. Their arrival meant the 1942 Chevrolet was turned into a reserve vehicle, and the 1935 Chevrolet was relegated to a utility or parade vehicle. (Photograph by Ernie Metcalfe.)

The Beaverton Rural Fire Protection District received this white Pirsch-Ford in 1962 shortly before the Beaverton Fire Department received its two red vehicles of the same make. This vehicle came with a 1,000-gallon-per-minute, two-stage, mid-ship Hale pump and a tank capable of holding 500 gallons. It would later be sent to Progress once that station was completed in 1965. (Photograph by Ernie Metcalfe.)

This too is a Pirsch-Ford pumper coming out of the downtown Beaverton station where it was stored. Beaverton Fire Department volunteers and paid firefighters also drove the Beaverton Rural Fire Protection District vehicles. (Photograph by Ernie Metcalfe.)

Bill Dalton (left), unidentified, and Cal McGann (right) practice a Beaverton Fire Department hose drill in the 1950s. A 1952 roster lists the paid personnel of the department as including McGann, Chief Archie Olson, and Harvey Williams. With the beginning of a paid department came a regular schedule from here on out: a 24-hour, on-duty shift followed by 48 hours off duty. (Photograph by Ernie Metcalfe.)

Beaverton Fire Department personnel attended a house-burning exercise conducted by the Oregon Fire Instruction Association outside of McMinnville in March 1963. As part of the exercise, firefighters used water from a dammed ditch, drawing it through a tanker to extinguish the blaze. (Photograph by Ernie Metcalfe.)

Beaverton firefighters, including Ben Kinkaid (on the running board with the horn) and Leo Wright (also on the running board), appear in the Rainier Days parade aboard the 1935 Chevrolet that was later used for salvage. On the hood is volunteer Lyle Ingram dressed as "Mis-Fire," according to his sash. (Photograph by Ernie Metcalfe.)

Beaverton Fire Department engineer and driver Frank Pohs (left) watches as Beaverton volunteer Capt. Joe Thomas (center) walks with Gordy Patchin (carrying the hose). They are participating in a joint drill with the West Slope Fire Department on Canyon Road at about 114th Avenue in 1964. (Photograph by Ernie Metcalfe.)

A firefighter from the Aloha Fire Department watches a house go up during a controlled burning exercise with the West Slope Fire Department on Canyon Road at about 114th Avenue in 1964. Formed in 1947, the Beaverton Rural Fire Protection District was once known as the Aloha Fire Department, and volunteers were located in a station on 185th Avenue across from the Aloha Post Office. The station is now a tavern, but the engine-bay doors of the building are still visible. (Photograph by Ernie Metcalfe.)

Rescue 6, a one-ton, 1968 Ford F-350 (shown here in the early 1970s) became the Beaverton Fire Department's first rescue vehicle. Originally equipped with an electronic siren, it was later replaced with a Federal Q-series siren that was louder, spreading sound waves over a larger distance. Up until this time, all of the department's engines were painted red. Rescue 6 was painted yellow for greater visibility, and all other department vehicles soon followed. The vehicle was never used to transport patients. (Photograph by Ernie Metcalfe.)

The main Beaverton Fire Station at Fifth Street and Hall Boulevard (above) closed in June 1999 after falling into disrepair. For more than 40 years, the structure, torn down the next month, served as the downtown station. Firefighters moved into the station, which was a part of the old Beaverton City Hall, in July 1958. The cost of the entire building was $250,000 with the fire station portion containing five bays, sleeping quarters, a kitchen, meeting room, and office space. In this July 8, 1999, photograph (below), all that remains is the large beam that spanned the width of the old fire station bay. The beam is believed to have been recycled into a table for one of the fire stations. (Both photographs by Ernie Metcalfe.)

Beaverton mayor Rob Drake and Tualatin Valley Fire & Rescue board member Carol Gearin cut a ribbon for the new downtown Beaverton Fire Station 67 on Farmington Road in 1999. The building was badly needed. Former Beaverton fire chief Oscar "Sox" Lee said the old station at Fifth Street and Hall Boulevard "leaked like a sieve" and even had mushrooms growing in it. (Photograph by Ernie Metcalfe.)

A 1950s natural gas explosion on the northwest corner of Seventh Street and Hall Boulevard in downtown Beaverton blew out the contents of the home onto the roof (a trunk and bed frame are visible). Miraculously, the two women inside "didn't even get scratched," according to Capt. Ernie Metcalfe, a former firemen and Beaverton Fire Department historian. The home was rebuilt and still stands today. (Photograph by Ernie Metcalfe.)

The yellow equipment that kept the Beaverton Fire Department going in the 1970s includes, from top to bottom, a 1962 Pirsch engine, Rescue 6 (the first dedicated rescue vehicle in the city), and a 1972 Mack truck with an elevated aerial platform. The vehicles here all ran out of the main Beaverton Station. (Courtesy of TVF&R.)

With Tualatin Rural Fire Protection District and Washington County Fire District No. 1 set to merge in the late 1980s (Beaverton would annex later), a new name was sought for the district. Three names emerged: "Consolidated," "Fanno Creek", and "Tualatin Valley." Because "Consolidated" looked like it would ultimately be the winner, some vehicles sported the moniker for about six months before the legal merger took place. "Tualatin Valley Fire & Rescue" emerged as the winning name. (Courtesy of TVF&R.)

This 1953 photograph of a training event at the main station of the Portland Fire Bureau is rare because it features several chiefs of area departments, including Bill Barngrover (second row, second from left), the first chief of the Tualatin Rural Fire Protection District; Warren Cravens (second row, far right), a captain for the Cedar Mill Fire District; Walt Unis (to Craven's left), a Beaverton Fire Department volunteer; George Kline (third row, leaning on the hood in the helmet), a Beaverton Fire Department volunteer; and George Foege (next to Kline in checkered jacket), chief of the Cedar Mill Rural Fire Protection District. (Photograph by Ernie Metcalfe.)

Volunteers from the Beaverton Rural Fire Protection District mop up a fire on Merlo Road in the late 1940s or early 1950s. On the roof are Clarance Buffam (left) and John Barnes. Buffam was assistant postmaster of the downtown Beaverton Post Office when it was located on First Street. (Photograph by Ernie Metcalfe.)

A tight shot of the Beaverton Fire Department's Rescue 6 from the early 1970s shows some of the tools of the trade. They include a Homelite XL-88 rescue saw with a metal-cutting disc. To the right of the saw is an Aero-Fog device, which produced a fine fog that got rid of the smell of smoke after a fire. The city of Tokoroa, New Zealand, was so impressed with Rescue 6 that it asked for the specifications to build one for its fire department. Going one better, former captain Ernie Metcalfe took pictures of every possible view of the vehicle. "They built one just like it," Metcalfe recalled. The rescue vehicle also contained lights, a four-way electrical box, ropes, and hydraulic jacks. (Photograph by Ernie Metcalfe.)

The 1962 Oregon Fire Chiefs' Convention, held at the Pilot Butte Inn in Bend, attracted several casually dressed attendees, including Hueston Reynolds (left), who at the time was chief of the West Slope Fire Department (only to be named Beaverton's chief a year later); Bob Wickam (center), Beaverton Fire Department chief; and Don Thomas, a volunteer captain. In 1963, the annual convention was held jointly by the Beaverton and West Slope Fire Departments. (Photograph by Ernie Metcalfe.)

This 1947 Dodge pumper used by the Beaverton Rural Fire Protection District had a 60-gallon-per-minute, high-pressure Bean pump. The engine would drive 600 pounds per square inch of water with what was essentially an agricultural pump used to spray orchards; it was capable of tearing off roof shingles or uprooting vegetation. (Photograph by Ernie Metcalfe.)

Members of the West Slope, Beaverton, and Cedar Mill Fire Departments practice putting out an oil fire during a training session at a Portland Fire Bureau facility in Linton in the mid-1960s. The three departments often joined together in practice burns and training. (Photograph by Ernie Metcalfe.)

Guy Carr (left), owner of Carr Chevrolet and a noted civic leader, poses with his mechanics and a Beaverton Fire Department truck in 1942. Carr, who arrived in Beaverton in 1919, was a volunteer fireman. When the city went broke during the Depression and water was cut off because the city could not pay the $75,000, Carr and other members of the Beaverton City Council signed a note that allowed them to drill their own well. (Courtesy of Beaverton Historical Society.)

Beaverton fire chief Bob Wickam (right) holds a sign lobbying to lure the 1963 state fire convention to the Beaverton/West Slope areas. He was successful, and events were held in such locations as Beaverton High School with meals served at St. Cecilia Catholic Church. To the left is West Slope chief Hueston Reynolds's Ford station wagon. (Photograph by Ernie Metcalfe.)

The two new Pirsch fire engines arrived in June 1962 and were proudly displayed in front of the main Beaverton station. They would initially be dubbed Engine 9 (left) and Engine 6. They were identical, except for a deck pipe installed aboard Engine 9, and each pumped 1,000 gallons per minute of water, doubling the pumping capacity of the old Dodge fire engines. They were the first pieces of new equipment purchased since the 1942 Chevrolet arrived during World War II. Although the Pirsches had a jump seat to ride in, many firefighters still rode on the tailgate. The vehicles were retrieved by Chief Bob Wickam and his wife, who traveled to Kenosha, Wisconsin, to pick up one of them. The other was brought back by firefighter Don Thomas and his wife. (Photograph by Ernie Metcalfe.)

Beaverton firefighters attend a crab feed in the Beaverton station in March 1963. They include, from left to right, Chief Bob Wickam, Harvey Williams, Evelyn Metcalfe, Ken Hunt, and Tom Moe. The crab feeds were a tradition Wickam had brought with him from his old department in Baker, Oregon. (Photograph by Ernie Metcalfe.)

Larry Godfrey climbs into Engine 266, located at the Brockman Road station, in the mid-1970s. This is one of the original Pirsch engines purchased by the Beaverton Fire Department in 1962. The change at this point is that the vehicle had been sent to Springfield, Oregon, for conversion into a turbo-charged, inline-6 diesel engine. Also, the old manual transmission was replaced with an automatic transmission. (Courtesy of TVF&R.)

Frank Oulman (left) and Justin George Jr. appear in front of Rescue 6, the first dedicated rescue vehicle for the Beaverton Fire Department. The bright-yellow vehicle was initially staffed by first aid–certified Red Cross personnel and later by EMTs. Oulman would become the Beaverton Fire Department's first emergency medical services director with Laird Blanchard becoming TVF&R's first emergency medical services director after the merger. (Courtesy of Frank Oulman.)

TVF&R displays its new rescue vehicles, which were purchased in the 1990s. The Beaverton vehicle (third from left) includes the department's distinctive yellow stripe. At the time, when standard ambulances were not available, the rescue vehicles could transport patients to the hospital. Since the beginning of fire departments answering emergency calls, the number of calls for such emergencies far outweighed the number of fire calls. (Photograph by Harvey Thomas, courtesy of Frank Oulman.)

Proudly posing in front of a 1947 Dodge Beaverton Rural Fire Protection District engine in this 1950s photograph are, from left to right, Alden Oleson, Oscar Hagg, Leland Flint, Chief Archie Olson, "Speedy" Clauson, and Assistant Chief Harvey Williams. This is one of two engines purchased by the Beaverton Fire Department after voters passed a bond measure. The vehicles could pump 500 gallons of water per minute. The rural fire protection engines shared quarters with city engines, all of which were parked at the main Beaverton station, located then at First and Angel Streets in Beaverton. (Courtesy of TVF&R.)

Beaverton's first hook and ladder company marches in a Fourth of July parade in 1901. The specifics on how official or organized the group was are unknown because a written record of Beaverton investing in firefighting equipment does not appear until 1919. Parade personnel include Earl Evans with the drum, Earl E. Fisher with the fife and bugle, Walter Chatterton with the cant hook, and Harry Summers (left front) with the ladder. (Courtesy of Beaverton Historical Society.)

Although no one is certain when this dramatic nighttime photograph was taken, it was most likely between 1931 and 1959. It shows a house or shack ablaze on Cooper Mountain and was taken approximately one-eighth of a mile from what is now the 16000 block of Southwest Satterburg Road. (Courtesy of Beaverton Historical Society.)

Two

Tualatin Rural Fire Protection District

Like so many early fire departments, the Tualatin Fire Department was first formed by a group of volunteers. In this case, it was on February 2, 1935.

A year later, the group would formally establish the Tualatin Fire Department, electing William "Bill" Barngrover as its chief. With fire hydrants already installed, a hose wagon was purchased, which relied on the manpower of volunteers to manually drag the cart to fires until a special hitch was crafted.

In the late 1930s, the city of Tualatin's first vehicle, a Federal fire engine, was purchased. From 1937–1946, Tualatin's city fire department was manned by volunteers. The second fire engine purchased was a converted 1930 Reo school bus, which was shipped to the area in a crate and assembled at a Portland automobile dealership.

In 1946, the Tualatin Rural Fire Protection District would officially form and a fire station was built that same year at Eighty-fourth Avenue and Seneca Street in downtown Tualatin. Barngrover was named chief of that organization as well. The Stafford-Wilsonville Rural Fire Protection District was organized two years later, contracting with Tualatin Rural for service and formally becoming part of the district several months later.

Meanwhile, Sherwood, Tualatin's neighbor to the west had been operating with a volunteer fire department since its early days. That changed on April 26, 1950, when two large fires burned a half block of Old Town Sherwood. On December 7, the remaining buildings on that block burned as well, except for the post office and a lone building on the corner.

As a result, Sherwood began the New Year contracting with Tualatin Rural Fire Protection District to provide service, a contract that would last until 1957. In 1968, Sherwood residents voted to annex into the rapidly growing fire district.

After a long, distinguished career spanning 30 years, Chief Barngrover retired in 1965, leaving Russ Washburn as the new chief. In 1967, an engine would be assigned to the district's new station in Wilsonville. That same year, a 100-foot American LaFrance aerial ladder was purchased for the rural district, a piece of equipment that would remain with the department until its sale for $5,000 in 1983. In 1982, the district's first female volunteer firefighter, Mary Nyssen, joined the district.

When former chief Bill Barngrover died in June 1970, his funeral procession snaked through the city of Tualatin, led by the last engine he officially purchased as chief. "He lived for it," his daughter Rita Barngrover would later say about her father's years in the fire service. "He used a lot of his own money to keep it going."

The era of the Tualatin Rural Fire Protection District would officially end in 1989, as the district merged with Washington County Fire District No. 1 to become Tualatin Valley Fire & Rescue. By that time, the Tualatin Rural Fire Protection District encompassed 125 square miles.

Firefighter Melvin Salzer (left) displays one of Tualatin Rural Fire Protection District's first trucks while William Barngrover Jr. (right) shows off another, a 1930 Reo school bus, which had its top removed. The vehicles are parked in front of the district's first fire station, located two doors down from what was then Clark's Lumber Company in Tualatin. (Rita Barngrover Conover collection, courtesy of Tualatin Historical Society.)

William Barngrover Jr., son of Tualatin Rural Fire Protection District chief William Barngrover, sits aboard the city of Tualatin's second fire engine, a converted 1930 Reo school bus. The bus was shipped in a crate and assembled at a Portland automobile dealership. (Rita Barngrover Conover collection, courtesy of Tualatin Historical Society.)

The first and second fire trucks, known as the Federal (left) and Red, sit parked in front of what was Tualatin's first city hall on Boone's Ferry Road. All the fire trucks were white in those days. Fire calls came into the home of Chief William Barngrover with a hand-cranked phone ringing and alerting volunteers through a siren. (Rita Barngrover Conover collection, courtesy of Tualatin Historical Society.)

The Tualatin Rural Fire Protection District displays a variety of its vehicles in front of the fire station, which was built in 1946. (Rita Barngrover Conover collection, courtesy of Tualatin Historical Society.)

Residents gather for an annual birthday party inside the bay of the fire station in the early 1950s. The Tualatin Rural Fire Protection District tried to hold the annual party as near as it could to February 2, the date in 1935 that the original fire department was founded by five volunteers: John Hiller, Roy Sagert, Cecil Ladd, Ed Robinson, and William Barngrover. (Rita Barngrover Conover collection, courtesy of Tualatin Historical Society.)

Construction on the new Tualatin Fire Station at Southwest Eighty-fourth Avenue and Seneca Street in Tualatin progresses in the mid-1940s. "It was all volunteer work," said Rita Barngrover Conover, daughter of Chief William Barngrover. On the top scaffolding (left) is volunteer firefighter Marion Maxwell with Chief Barngrover (back to photographer) overseeing the work. Volunteers from the original Tualatin Fire Department formed a new, separate, incorporated organization apart from the city that owned the land the station sat upon, working for $1 per hour to keep costs low. (Rita Barngrover Conover collection, courtesy of Tualatin Historical Society.)

Tualatin Rural Fire Protection District firefighters display all their vehicles in front of the downtown station. They include an unidentified firefighter (left), Guy Scull (center), and Merwyn Conover. (Rita Barngrover Conover collection, courtesy of Tualatin Historical Society.)

From left to right, Leonard Wilcutt, Floyd Berning, Marion "Dutch" Maxwell, Chief William Barngrover, Cliff Floyd, and Wilbur Nyberg stand in front of the chief's car in the late 1940s or early 1950s. Accompanying them is Dottie, the firehouse Dalmatian. (Rita Barngrover Conover collection, courtesy of Tualatin Historical Society.)

Posing on Tigard's Main Street in 1955 are members of the Tualatin Rural Fire Protection District. This same year, a gigantic fundraising effort was launched to build a fire station, community center, and space for the Tigard Water District. The project bogged down but was restarted by Ivan Jack with enough money collected to finish the project in 1957. (Courtesy of the Tualatin Historical Society.)

The B-shift in the main station of Tualatin Rural Fire Protection District in May 1970 includes, from left to right, Lt. Guy Skull, firefighter Larry Tracy, student volunteer Gary Toll, alarm operator Jack Heironymous, and engineer John Swartz with Engine 22. Peeking out from inside the bay are the volunteer engine that ended up at the Wilsonville Station (left) and First Aid 23. (Courtesy of Gary Toll.)

In May 1970, Gary Toll and Sparky, the Tualatin Rural Fire Protection District's mascot, sit aboard an old Federal engine used as a parade rig. Sparky, owned by Capt. Joe Greulich, was used in fire prevention demonstrations. Toll described the dog as very well trained, laid-back, and friendly. (Courtesy of Gary Toll.)

The extensive, early Tualatin Rural Fire Protection District apparatus is on display. The district would install its first 30-watt, two-way radios in three of its engines in April 1949. That same year, money was donated to allow the district to purchase a first-aid car, a Chevrolet panel truck. (Courtesy of TVF&R.)

Firefighters stand at attention during the funeral of Tualatin Rural Fire Protection District's first chief, William Barngrover, in the summer of 1970. In the image above, they include, from left to right, Dennis Messman (an alarm operator), Larry Etzel, Phil Lapp, and Lt. Gene Chamberlain. "Everyone I talked to just thought he was a good person to work for," recalled his daughter Rita Barngrover Conover. A newspaper photograph of the procession showed the final engine that the chief had purchased before his retirement, Engine 208. The newspaper reported that the funeral included "uniformed men, polished equipment on review at stations in Tigard and Tualatin. Siren sounded full cycle at grave site." In the image below, from left to right are Chamberlain, Lapp, Etzel, and Messman in front of the station as the funeral cortege passes. (Both, courtesy of Gary Toll.)

Firefighters from Tualatin Rural Fire Protection District took this photograph looking east from the 90-foot aerial truck in December 1969. Vehicles on display in front of the fire department include, from left to right, the Ford engine used by volunteers, Engine 22 (the Ford that could pump 1,500 gallons per minute), First Aid No. 23 (an old Cadillac), and the chief's car. (Courtesy of Gary Toll.)

Engine 223 (left), a 1966 Ford that was assigned to Sherwood, and Engine 233, also a part of Sherwood's volunteer engine company, respond to a nighttime barn fire in rural Sherwood in September 1970. (Courtesy of Sherwood Volunteer Firefighters' Association.)

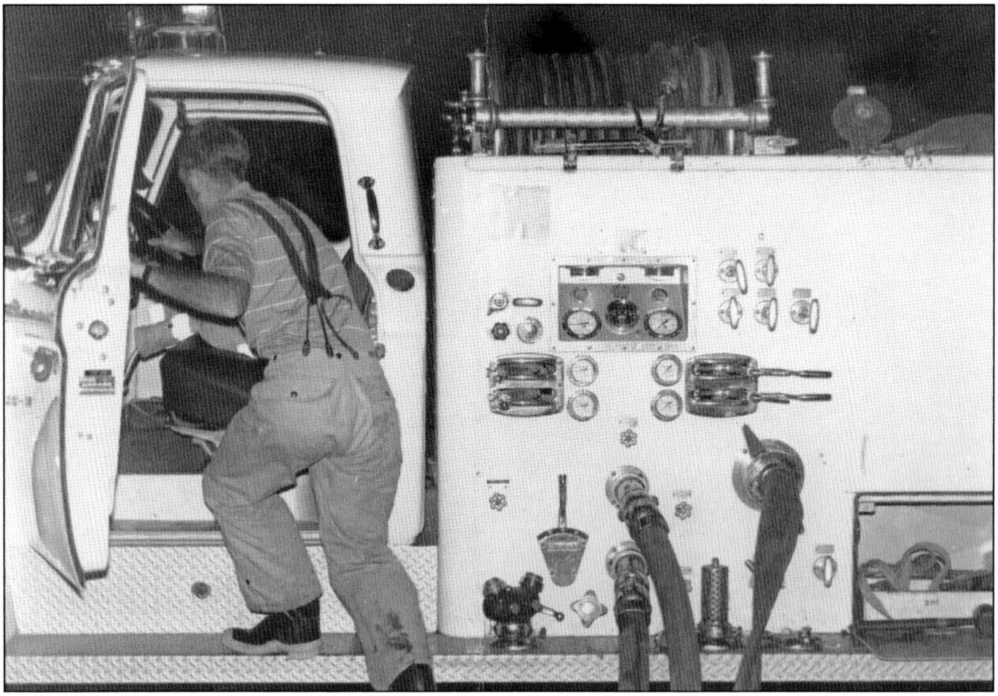

Firefighter Barney Davis enters Engine 223 during a September 1970 rural Sherwood barn fire. The ability to fight fires in Sherwood became political on April 26, 1950, when a blaze destroyed a half-block of Old Town Sherwood. The remaining block burned on December 7, 1950, leaving only the old post office and another building. Although the city had a volunteer fire department, it decided to contract with the Tualatin Rural Fire Protection District on January 1, 1951. (Courtesy of Sherwood Volunteer Firefighters' Association.)

A Tualatin Rural Fire Protection District firefighter battles a barn blaze in rural Sherwood in September 1970. In 1957, the city terminated its contract with the Tualatin Rural Fire Protection District and reactivated its volunteer department. That would last until 1968 when Sherwood voters approved annexing into the Tualatin Rural Fire Protection District. (Courtesy of Sherwood Volunteer Firefighters' Association.)

Engine 233, a 1966 Ford T-850, sits in the bay of the Sherwood Fire Station. Designed to fight grass fires, the five-speed vehicle was a little tricky to drive, according to one engineer. (Courtesy of Sherwood Volunteer Firefighters' Association.)

Construction on the new Sherwood Fire Station on Oregon Street began in July 1970. Numerous firefighters worked on getting the new building up and running. In the three years before it was completed, the Sherwood Fire Department responded to 10 fires, 11 false alarms, and 41 calls for mutual aid to other departments. (Courtesy of Sherwood Volunteer Firefighters' Association.)

Engine 253 out of the Progress station (left) passes the fully engulfed Lawrenz Building on the corner of First and Pine Streets in Sherwood in the mid- to late 1980s. Over the years, the building had been home to a variety of businesses, including a restaurant. In 1916, it opened as the site of Lawrenz's Garage, a Ford dealership owned by Emil Lawrenz. Lawrenz, who sold 61 Fords in 1928, would teach customers to drive with every car sold. Below, firefighters battle the same fire. The former Robin Hood Theater, a building that was later torn down because of seismic concerns, is still standing (to the right of the burning structure) at the time of the blaze. (Both, courtesy of Sherwood Volunteer Firefighters' Association.)

Tualatin Rural Fire Protection District firefighter Gary Toll cools off some hot lumber during a fire at the Conrad Smeltzer place in Sherwood in May 1971. In addition to nine full-time firefighters and fifteen volunteers from the Tualatin District, nine firefighters from Washington County Fire District No. 2 (the Midway station at Scholls) were sent to this blaze. Loss to the house was estimated at $12,000 with another $3,000 of contents reported. (Photograph by Jerry Crume, courtesy of Sherwood Volunteer Firefighters' Association.)

Engine 223 from Tualatin Rural Fire Protection District (above) shoots water on Sherwood's Frontier Leather Company on September 25, 1981. The fire caused about $700,000 in damage to the building, including a loss of $200,000 in leather projects. "The fire department did a hell of a good job; they saved the main part of the building," manager Don Nelson told a reporter for the *Tigard/Tualatin Times* newspaper. The three-alarm blaze resulted in the collapse of part of the tannery roof and destroyed a leather-drying room and shipping area. At the height of the blaze, flames shot an estimated 150 feet into the air. A total of 60 fighters from Tualatin Rural Fire Protection District, Washington County Fire Districts 1 and 2, Portland Fire Bureau, and Lake Oswego, Beaverton, and Canby Fire Departments all helped to extinguish the fire. During the blaze, two firefighters received minor injuries. (Both, courtesy of Sherwood Volunteer Firefighters' Association.)

Woody Woodhouse, a volunteer and Tualatin Rural Fire Protection District board member, stands in front of a snorkel in April 1970. When not engaging in firefighting activities, Woodhouse worked at his business, Woody's Bakery, in Sherwood. He was named Fireman of the Year in 1970. (Courtesy of Sherwood Volunteer Firefighters' Association.)

A Sherwood Fire Department engine sits in front of quarters the fire department shared with the community's first city hall (the front facade was built in 1893) and the public library on Main Street. The building was torn down in the early 1980s. (Courtesy of TVF&R.)

Tualatin Rural Fire Protection District firefighters and volunteers from Sherwood (above) fight a fire at the Sherwood United Methodist Church at Third and Main Streets on March 19, 1976. Below, two firefighters ventilate the roof aboard an aerial fire truck out of Tigard. The building, which was constructed in 1893, had to be razed, according to Sherwood historian Clyde List. Still, the two cedar trees seen in the photograph above survived the fire. Also, the church bell and some of the church pews were saved and moved to the new Sherwood United Methodist Church on Washington Street in Sherwood. (Both, courtesy of Sherwood Volunteer Firefighters' Association.)

Engine 233 responds to a two-alarm fire at the farm of Jerry Bitz on Heater Road on August 17, 1976. The area proved to be a hot spot with another major brush fire reported on Heater Road on September 6, 1981, when a three-alarm fire required mutual aid responses from eight departments. (Courtesy of Sherwood Volunteer Firefighters' Association.)

On October 11, 1974, one of the larger fires for the Tualatin Rural Fire Protection District occurred at Bischof Farms. The four-alarm fire was at Brown Road, about 1,000 feet east of Grahams Ferry Road. Lost in the fire was a potato storage warehouse containing thousands of pounds of potatoes and onions. (Courtesy of Sherwood Volunteer Firefighters' Association.)

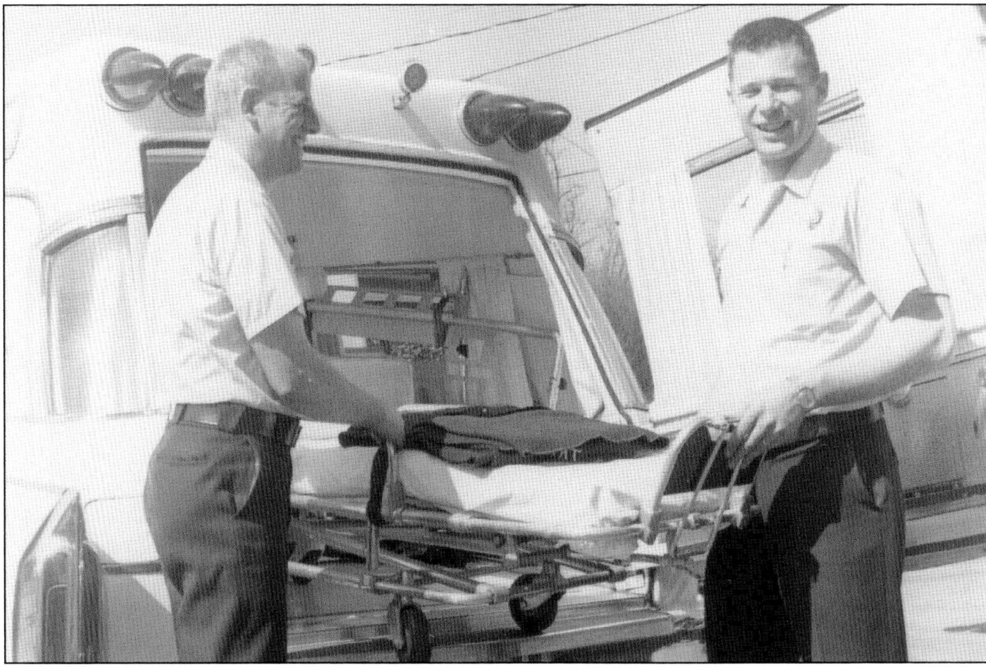

In the image above, Gordon Scott (left) and Phil Lapp place a gurney in a Tualatin Rural Fire Protection District ambulance, a 1966 Cadillac, in front of the main Tualatin station in 1969. The vehicle, which reportedly "drove fast," was the third fully equipped ambulance the district owned. Below, Scott and Lapp get into the vehicle. The pair worked for the district from 1968 through 1993. District ambulance service was suspended on July 1, 1972. In 1974, Rescue 22 went into service, becoming the district's first paramedic unit. (Both, courtesy of Sherwood Volunteer Firefighters' Association.)

During a January 1974 flood, a lone fire sedan sits in front of Tualatin Rural Fire Protection District's main station, which was located then at Southwest Eighty-fourth Avenue and Seneca Street. The station was later torn down, and a parking lot sits in its place with the Winona Grange behind it. (Courtesy of Sherwood Volunteer Firefighters' Association.)

Following the flood on January 18, 1974, Tualatin Rural Fire Protection District battalion chief Joe Greulich (right) floats in a raft with an unidentified friend in front of the Hedges Creek apartments he owned on Boones Ferry Road in Tualatin. Much of the downtown area was covered with water the day after when this photograph was taken. (Photograph by Dennis Messman, courtesy of Sherwood Volunteer Firefighters' Association.)

Gary Meacham (left) and two other members of Tualatin Rural Fire Protection District pump water out of a ditch next to the K-mart parking lot in Tualatin following the January 18, 1974, flood. While the downtown area remained covered in water, a sandbag dike installed on both sides of Boones Ferry Road created limited dry space on portions of the roadway. (Courtesy of Sherwood Volunteer Firefighters' Association.)

Volunteer firefighter Calvin "Cap" Kruse, a volunteer firefighter with Tualatin Rural Fire Protection, uses a yardstick to measure the several inches of water that remained in front of the fire station at Southwest Eighty-fourth Avenue and Seneca Street in Tualatin following the January 18, 1974, flood. Rains raised the Tualatin River to the highest levels in 20 years, causing it to overflow its banks. (Courtesy of Sherwood Volunteer Firefighters' Association.)

An old patch from the Sherwood Volunteer Fire Department gives a nod to Robin Hood, often identified with the city of Sherwood. Volunteers have long played an important part in the district's fire history. In July 1967, the Sherwood Volunteer Firefighters' Association was formed. The group came up with a recipe for barbecued chicken that has been a hit at city events and festivals for 40 years. (Courtesy of TVF&R.)

Engine 223, based in Sherwood, drives past the Mountain Home United Methodist Church in July 1984. Fire officials suspected arson was the reason for the blaze that burned the building, and a $5,000 reward was offered for information leading to an arrest. Damage was estimated at as much as $300,000 at the time. Built in 1953 and located at Mountain Home and Le Beau Roads, the church had replaced a previous church that was destroyed by fire. (Courtesy of Sherwood Volunteer Firefighters' Association.)

Tualatin Rural Fire Protection District's American LaFrance aerial ladder truck was a 100-foot piece of equipment that had to be housed in a separate building across the street from the old Tualatin fire station after being purchased in 1967. The snorkel was capable of aiding firefighters should anything happen at the old multistoried Farmer's Insurance building at Highway 217 and Interstate 5, the tallest building in the fire district at that time. (Courtesy of Gary Toll.)

Gary Toll began his career with Tualatin Rural Fire Protection District in 1969 as a "sleeper," a volunteer who had a day job but slept in the fire station at night. He was hired by the district in 1971 and promoted to engineer three years later. He later served aboard Rescue 22 based in Tualatin, one of the first paramedic fire department units in the state. Later, he would work on the district's hazardous materials unit and finished his career as a fire marshal.

Three

Washington County Fire District No. 1

Washington County Fire District No. 1 had its beginnings in the old Beaverton Rural Fire Protection District, which was started in 1947 to provide fire protection to the Aloha area. Before that time, only one engine (stored in a garage in Aloha) was responsible for protecting the area. In general, the community and volunteers referred to the district as the Aloha Fire Department.

In 1950, the Aloha station was built on 185th Avenue. The bay doors of the abandoned station are still visible, and the building has been turned into a tavern. In 1961, the district hired Walt Platt as its first paid employee, replacing volunteer chief George Dimeo.

Because a large part of the fire district was on the east side of Beaverton, a contract was signed between the City of Beaverton and the Beaverton Rural Fire Protection District. As a result, the district's two engines were staffed by city personnel and housed in Beaverton's main downtown station. Platt served as fire chief of the rural fire district from 1965 to 1972.

In 1972, Cedar Mill and West Slope Fire Protection Districts merged under the umbrella of Washington County Fire District No. 1. (Local residents often referred to those entities as either the Cedar Hill or West Slope Fire Departments.) Platt was subsequently named fire chief of Washington County Fire District No. 1, a position he held from 1972 to 1983.

Until 1942, fire protection in the Cedar Mill area was generally provided by Beaverton. Local residents George Foege and Dave Ediger took it upon themselves to form the Cedar Mill Fire Patrol, which became the Cedar Mill Rural Fire Protection District in 1946. Foege became chief, a position he held until his retirement in 1972.

For Foege and Ediger, the first order of business was transforming a one-and-a-half-ton 1936 Chevrolet pickup truck (secured from the Oregon Truck Wrecking Company) into the district's first fire truck. In 1947, property was purchased along Cornell Road for a fire station. The station was a two-story building that included an upstairs sleeping room. It remained a working fire station until its closure in June 1984, and as of this writing, it houses an automobile-related business with the old hose towers still visible.

Meanwhile, the West Slope Rural Fire Protection District had similar beginnings. Prior to 1941, residents of West Slope had to rely on an old converted Dodge school bus for fire service. The first meeting of the West Slope Rural Fire Protection District's board of directors was on March 3, 1949, where board members took up their first items of business after area voters had agreed to the district's formation a year earlier.

In the summer of 1950, the first West Slope fire engine arrived, a 1951 International equipped with a 600-gallon-per-minute pump and the capacity to carry 400 gallons of water. The fully equipped vehicle was purchased from Hillsboro Sales Company for $16,000. The board of directors now needed a fire station and eventually found a parcel at the intersection of what is now Eighty-seventh Avenue and Canyon Drive. The board snapped up the property in March 1953 for a price tag of $9,000. In 2006, TVF&R voters approved replacing the outdated station.

Washington County Fire District No. 1 firefighter Mike Hart peers out from one of the district's older engines in the early 1970s. He is parked at the old Aloha station on 185th Avenue, which was located across the street from the post office and is now occupied by a tavern. (Photograph by Steve May.)

An early 1960s Cadillac ambulance (right) is displayed in front of the Raleigh Hills Safeway store. The ambulance, which was housed at the Aloha Fire Station, was allowed to transport patients to the hospital at the time. It was purchased and maintained by donations collected from the sale of tickets to the annual firefighters dance held at the Kinton Grange on Scholls Ferry Road. To the left of the ambulance is the 1969 West Slope Rescue 1. (Photograph by Harvey Thomas, courtesy of TVF&R.)

Bystanders watch a fire on Southwest Rachelle Court in April 1977 as Lee Coleman, public information officer for Washington County Fire District No. 1 (with clipboard), gets a few answers. To the right is the 90-foot snorkel truck that once was housed in the Jenkins Road station. (Photograph by Harvey Thomas, courtesy of TVF&R.)

Dave Marks (left) practices in Haag Lake with an unidentified Newberg firefighter in 1985 as part of Washington County Fire District No. 1's dive team. The impetus for the team came after two young people were found clinging to a bush in the Rock Creek Golf Course after Rock Creek overflowed its banks. According to retired firefighter Capt. Duane Watt, rescue was undertaken with ropes but without life jackets. An initial call for firefighters interested in serving on the dive team attracted 36 volunteers. (Courtesy of TVF&R.)

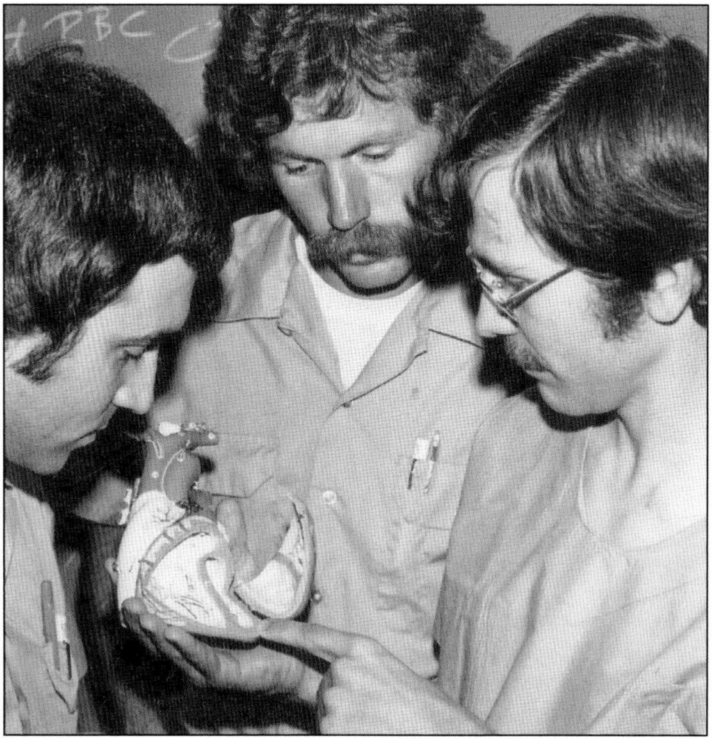

Steve McCarthy (left) and Skip Labisch receive cardiac training from a physician at St. Vincent Hospital inside the Progress Fire Station around 1975. The Progress Station was opened in 1966 with a newspaper reporting that plans were to operate with a six-man team and one truck. The goal was to expand the station, which was then part of the Beaverton Rural Fire Protection District, once money became available. (Courtesy of TVF&R.)

New Washington County Fire District No. 1 firefighters are completing training in 1979 at what was then the district's administration headquarters on Blanton Street. They include, from left to right, (first row) Rob Schneider, Mike Morton, Bob Kreipe, John Brett, and Phil Augustyn; (second row) Greg Grenfel, Rob DeHaan, Harold Weaver, Bob Singley, Dave Brown, John Aarness, and Bruce Averitt. (Courtesy of TVF&R.)

Early members of the Beaverton Rural Fire Protection District gather for a photograph. They include, from left to right, (first row) John Rohrbach, Gail Kilgore, Don Dehaan, Chief George Dimeo, Tommy Jones, Don Kirkman, Fred Kahler, and Cy Kirkland; (second row) Claude Gaunt, Arbie Kellas, Joe Berger, Jim Dickey, Bud Nault, Glen Pratt, Roy Berg, and Billy Little; (third row) Ivan Bernard and John McCrow. (Courtesy of TVF&R.)

Vehicles are parked in front of the old Aloha Fire Station located at 185th Avenue and Blanton Street in 1977. Its construction was the result of a large fire in 1947. According to an article in the October 27, 1976, *Aloha Breeze*, "The disaster awakened the community to the need for water, firefighters and equipment." A volunteer department was formed in October 1948. That department lasted only a brief time before the Beaverton Rural Fire Protection District took its place. (Photograph by Harvey Thomas, courtesy of TVF&R.)

A firefighter douses flames during a June 1983 fire at what was then known as Beaverton Mall II off Jenkins Road. The fire destroyed four businesses, and the owner of one of those was later charged with arson. The three-alarm fire brought firefighters from the Beaverton Fire Department, Washington County Fire District No. 1, and the Tualatin Rural Fire Protection District. The *Beaverton Valley Times* newspaper reported that the heat from the fire cracked the windshield of a District No. 1 truck and melted an overhead light in the vehicle. (Photograph by Harvey Thomas, courtesy of TVF&R.)

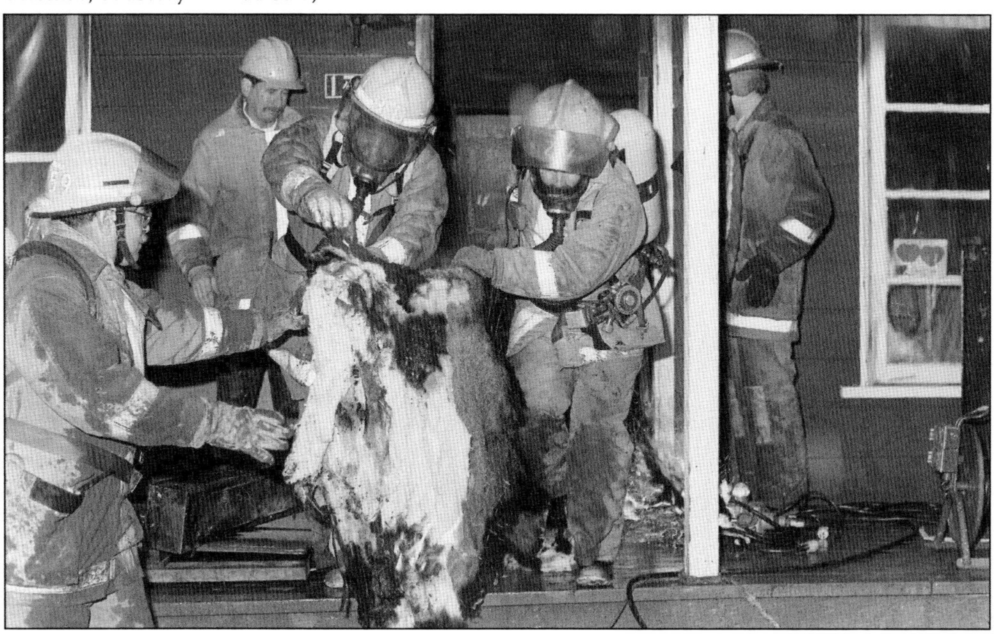

Washington County Fire District No. 1 firefighters remove debris following a house fire in the 17000 block of Johnson Street in November 1984. (Photograph by Harvey Thomas, courtesy of TVF&R.)

Washington County Fire District No. 1 firefighters, including volunteer Capt. Dave Gilbertson (center), put out debris during a house fire in the 17000 block of Johnson Street in November 1984. (Photograph by Harvey Thomas, courtesy of TVF&R.)

Washington County Fire District (WCFD) No. 1 firefighters successfully resuscitate four dogs at a home in the 4900 block of Southwest 180th Avenue on September 17, 1985. At least 20 firefighters from WCFD No. 1 and the Beaverton Fire Department responded to the scene to find smoke pouring from under the roof's eaves and flames shooting out of the home. After finding the four dogs, they gave them oxygen; the animals were later reported in good condition. (Photograph by Harvey Thomas, courtesy of TVF&R.)

Washington County Fire District No. 1 firefighter Gary Walters (above) puts water on one of several brush fires (and one barn fire) on August 8, 1981, as an aerial apparatus from Station 267 helps (below). That day, the district fought four blazes in the Germantown, Kaiser, and West Union Roads areas, hampered in large part by 106-degree heat and stiff breezes. Also aiding in the effort were crews from Washington County Fire District No. 2, Multnomah County Fire District No. 20, and the Portland Fire Bureau. In 1995, Multnomah County Fire District No. 20 (Skyline) would merge with Tualatin Valley Fire & Rescue. The area originally served sparsely populated farmland and forestland with rolling fields and deep ravines; fire service came from either Portland or Cedar Mill. (Both photographs by Harvey Thomas, courtesy of TVF&R.)

Washington County Fire District No. 1 firefighters battle an apartment fire in the 17000 block of Southwest Kinnaman Road on October 11, 1984. A youngster playing with matches on a couch was deemed the likely cause, an official said at the time. The blaze gutted one apartment and damaged two others. (Photograph by Harvey Thomas, courtesy of TVF&R.)

A firefighter sprays water on a vent following a house fire in the 8500 block of Southwest Cedarcrest Street in Metzger on April 12, 1982. A 20-year-old woman who was returning to her home saw flames shooting out from a family room. She crawled through a hallway filled with smoke and rescued her sleeping mother and grandmother. (Photograph by Harvey Thomas, courtesy of TVF&R.)

Washington County Fire District No. 1 firefighters battle a blaze. In 1972, Cedar Mill, West Slope, and Washington County Fire District No. 1 merged but retained the latter department's name. The new district took a progressive role in providing paramedic services to its coverage area with clinical training provided at St. Vincent Hospital. (Photograph by Harvey Thomas, courtesy of TVF&R.)

A Washington County Fire District No. 1 engine pokes out of the old Cedar Mill station at 129th Avenue and Cornell Road in 1973. The old station closed in June 1984 and is currently home to an automotive-related business with the hose tower still visible. (Photograph by Harvey Thomas, courtesy of TVF&R.)

Washington County Fire District No. 1 firefighters (right) battle a barn fire on Southwest 209th Avenue on April 11, 1982. Below, helping douse the flames are Dick Buchanan (left), an unidentified firefighter (center), and Dave Sellers. (Both photographs by Harvey Thomas, courtesy of TVF&R.)

Tom McKinney (right), an engineman with the Washington County Fire District No. 1 Explorers, leads a pump training session for fellow explorers, including Rob DeHann, (second from right) and unidentified explorers in the mid-1970s at the Somerset Fire Station on 185th Avenue. The explorer program was known for its high-quality curriculum with estimates that half of those who finished went on to become career firefighters. (Courtesy of TVF&R.)

Don Holland, the first hazardous materials (HazMat) specialist for Washington County Fire District No. 1, poses in front of a barrel of chemicals in 1987. "If it smelled bad, they called me," said Holland, who was a deputy fire marshal with the district. The district would soon form an official HazMat team. (Photograph by Harvey Thomas, courtesy of TVF&R.)

Firefighter Pat Raney (right), of Washington County Fire District No. 1, stands in front of Truck 252, an aerial vehicle, after helping rescue two hot-air balloonists and their pilot who became stuck on a light pole near Highways 217 and 26 on April 7, 1986. The ladder on the aerial proved about five feet too short (below) of its target, but members of the 304th Air Rescue Squadron eventually were able to reach the balloonists. It took four hours because a road consisting of 121 yards of gravel and 44 sheets of plywood had to be constructed. (Both photographs by Harvey Thomas, courtesy of TVF&R.)

Located in a 1970 ranch-style home on 147th Place, Station 68 will soon be only a memory. The last station in the district to be located in a home is set for replacement soon. (Photograph by Harvey Thomas, courtesy of TVF&R.)

From left to right, firefighter Rick Hopkins, firefighter Steve May, engineer Mike Hart, and Lt. Earl Frank, all from Washington County Fire District No. 1, pose during a lighter moment at the old Aloha station. By 1980, the station was abandoned and the district was taking bids (the lowest acceptable bid being $160,000) to sell the building. (Courtesy of Steve May.)

Phil Nelson (center) and Earl Reynolds (right), firefighters for Washington County Fire District No. 1, help pull a hose to hook up to a pump in the early 1970s. The fire district once covered 77 square miles, and after its merger with Cedar Mill and West Slope fire protection districts in 1972, it became the second largest fire district in the state at that time. (Photograph by Steve May.)

Tom Shriver became chief of the West Slope Rural Fire Protection District in 1963 after its first chief, Hueston Reynolds, left to take a job as chief of the Beaverton Fire Department. Shriver was a captain and training officer at the time. In January 1972, the West Slope district would merge with the Cedar Mill fire district and Washington County Fire District No. 1 with all of them taking the name of the latter district. (Photograph by Harvey Thomas, courtesy of TVF&R.)

Washington County Fire District No. 1 firefighter Steve May poses in front of Truck 221, a Seagraves truck with an aerial ladder, at the Tigard Fire Station, which was then located on Commercial Street in 1989. Since this was the same year as the merger with Tualatin Valley Fire & Rescue, the vehicle still has its old Tualatin Rural Fire Protection District logo. (Courtesy of Steve May.)

Members of the HazMat team, which was based out of the Progress station at that time, appear in the late 1980s or early 1990s. They include, from left to right, Terry Bowman, Mike Reed, Jeff Cooper, Bill Lovell, Terry Kline, Rick Burris, Gene Waibel, and Steve Balsiger. (Courtesy of TVF&R.)

Above, Joe Kust (center, with both arms on his hips), an alarm operator with Washington County Fire District No. 1 who worked at the Jenkins Road alarm center, visits the Portland alarm office in the 1970s. Below, alarm operators Ron Nodlund (left) and Bob Fryer were also part of those operators who fielded calls at the Jenkins Road station between 1971 and 1985. Those operations were later turned over to the Washington County Consolidated Communications Agency (WCCCA). Currently, WCCCA provides emergency dispatching for 18 fire and law enforcement agencies. (Both photographs by Harvey Thomas, courtesy of TVF&R.)

In 1963, West Slope firefighters demonstrate techniques near the station at Eighty-seventh Avenue and Canyon Drive as amused bystanders look on. This same year, West Slope chief Hueston Reynolds resigned to take a similar position with the city of Beaverton. Tom Shriver, a captain and training officer, was named to replace Reynolds. (Courtesy of TVF&R.)

West Slope firefighters scale a ladder during a January 1962 training fire off Southwest Broadway Street in Beaverton. At least 50 firefighters attended the training session. West Slope terminated its contract for service from Beaverton at the end of 1959. The district's first station located at Eighty-seventh Avenue and Canyon Drive opened in 1960. (Courtesy of TVF&R.)

Elmer Ward, a volunteer at the West Slope station, speaks into a tape recorder in the early 1960s. By the end of 1960, the growing department had 24 volunteers. (Courtesy of TVF&R.)

This 1951 International, shown in front of the West Slope station in 1962, could pump 600 gallons per minute and had a 400-gallon tank. Purchased for $16,000, the vehicle initially was housed at the downtown Beaverton station and manned by Beaverton firefighters until the West Slope station was opened in 1960. (Courtesy of TVF&R.)

Fire officials pose with Oregon governor Tom McCall (center) as he signs the Fire Standards and Accreditation Board Bill in the late 1960s. They include, from left to right, Walt Stickney (the state's fire marshal), West Slope chief Tom Shriver, two unidentified, Tualatin Rural Fire Protection District Chief Russ Washburn, two unidentified, George Howland (from East Multnomah Fire District No. 10), and unidentified. (Courtesy of TVF&R.)

An unidentified firefighter (left), Will Raines (center), and Bob Fryer stand outside the West Slope station with the 1951 International (used by the Beaverton Rural Fire Protection District to respond to fire calls in Progress and the surrounding rural areas) and the 1960 American LaFrance that included a soft-top roof. (Courtesy of TVF&R.)

Firefighters work on a January 1962 house fire in the West Slope Fire Department coverage area. Prior to 1941, West Slope residents had to rely on the City of Beaverton for fire protection with city volunteers responding to fires with a converted Dodge school bus complete with a 150-gallon-per-minute Edwards pump. In 1949, voters approved establishment of the West Slope Rural Fire Protection District.

From left to right, West Slope firefighters Dave Fox, Chuck LeBrun, Bob Armstrong, Bob Singley, Bob Kreipe, and Craig Keys celebrate receiving a Station Shift of the Year award at the West Slope station around 1980.

This West Slope Fire Department salvage rescue first-aid vehicle—a 1957 Chevrolet panel truck that was once used to deliver meat for a local company—is believed to be one of the first rescue vehicles in Washington County. West Slope firefighters used the truck, shown here in front of the station in 1963, for salvage gear at a time before they acquired a ladder truck. Designated as Squad 1 with radio call number 53, the vehicle carried such gear as a first-aid kit, stretchers, splints, and a resuscitator. Other equipment included 5- and 10-ton hydraulic jacks and electric fans used to clear smoke out of homes and buildings. (Courtesy of TVF&R.)

John Robinson (left), fire marshal for the West Slope Rural Fire Protection District, helps a student try on a mask for a fire breathing apparatus during a field trip to the station in the 1960s. In the background is the district's 1960 American LaFrance convertible (meaning it had a cloth top that could be removed as needed) engine. In fact, the rig was used to manufacture a hard-top version of the engine for the Elmira, New York–based American LaFrance company. (Courtesy of TVF&R.)

A 1967 American LaFrance Quint with an 85-foot ladder sits in front of the West Slope Fire Department in 1968. The vehicle, which contained a 1,500-gallon-per-minute pump, was fitted with remote operation of the bed-ladder pipe, compliments of Tom Thompson. Meanwhile, Larry Ekberg had a hand in the electrical operation of the bed-ladder and tip-ladder pipes.

Above, West Slope firefighters battle a four-alarm blaze at the Ortho Building at Canyon Road and Eighty-seventh Avenue in the 1960s. The fire station is located directly behind the building, and firefighters used a hydrant adjacent to the station to extinguish the blaze, according to Lee Coleman, a retired public information officer for Washington County Fire District No. 1. Firefighters used this 65-foot aerial ladder, which Beaverton purchased from Portland for $1, to fight the fire. The black semicircle toward the front of the fire truck is a net, which Coleman said was never used. However, the device was tested during training exercises at the Jenkins Road Tektronix building when volunteers jumped into it from a second-floor window. The cause of the fire was believed to have been the spontaneous combustion of rags. Below, a police officer oversees traffic during firefighting efforts at the building. (Both, courtesy of TVF&R.)

In 1942, Cedar Mill chief George Foege, along with Dave Ediger, helped organize the Cedar Mill Fire Patrol, which soon became the Cedar Mill Rural Fire Protection District. Foege would serve as its chief until 1972. "He treated his employees like they were gold," said retired Capt. Duane Watt. Watt said Foege was a respected, old-school chief. "Foege probably had more positive influences on young firefighters then anyone I've ever known," he said. (Courtesy of TVF&R.)

Aboard the Cedar Mill Rural Fire Protection District's first engine, a 1936 Chevrolet, firefighters prepare for an appearance in the 1967 Merrykana Parade in Portland. They include Dick Schmidt (on front bumper), Ed Wunderlich (left), Bill Doty (on hood), and Eldon Hart (right), as Gerald Thomas (fist raised) pretends to give John Glover a helmet knock. (Photograph by Carole Schmidt, courtesy of *Cedar Mill News*.)

Garland Duckworth, an engineer with the West Slope Fire Department, enjoys a bite of cake inside the station in October 1966. The different sized bell helmets in the background are equipped with an old bubble shield that was tinted yellow to allow firefighters to distinguish smoke from steam. According to former Washington County Fire District No. 1 public information officer Lee Coleman, West Slope conducted tests for the helmet manufacturer, even going so far as running over it with an engine. Below, Captain Larry Ekberg (left) and Engineer Lowell Peterson take time out to pose for a photograph at the West Slope Fire Station, also in 1966. (Both, courtesy of TVF&R.)

This 1969 Ford Super Van replaced the 1957 truck that served as one of the first rescue vehicles in Washington County. West Slope volunteer firefighters pitched in $1,200 to aid in the purchase of the new vehicle. (Courtesy of TVF&R.)

The West Slope Fire Department salvage rescue first-aid vehicle served the department well for many years. Purchased in 1963 by the West Slope Volunteer Firemen's Association, the 1957 Chevrolet panel truck was paid for with money collected through proceeds from the annual firemen's ball and from public donations. (Courtesy of TVF&R.)

Below, firefighters from Washington County Fire District No. 1 attend to a pilot whose single-engine Cessna 150 clipped the roof of a vacant, two-story home in the 1700 block of Sumac Lane on December 10, 1979. After striking the roof, the plane flipped backwards, landing in the front yard of the Aloha-area home near 179th Avenue and Farmington Road. The 44-year-old pilot was headed for the Hillsboro Airport when tower operators heard a Mayday distress call. Two bystanders pulled the pilot out of the plane and onto a wing after noticing there was flight fuel all around the plane. The victim was taken to an area hospital for treatment. (Both photographs by Harvey Thomas, courtesy of TVF&R.)

A firefighter from Washington County Fire District No. 1 (above) ventilates a roof on Thompson Road in unincorporated Washington County on January 11, 1978, as fellow firefighters (below) put out the fire. The homeowner said she heard a popping sound and saw flames and heavy smoke when she opened a door that contained a stairway leading to the attic. Four engines, one truck, one rescue vehicle, and eighteen firefighters responded to the incident, which resulted in an initial damage estimate of $2,500. Residents of the home had lived there for almost 30 years. (Both photographs by Mike Fletcher, courtesy of TVF&R.)

A Washington County Fire District No. 1 firefighter breaks a window to ventilate a four-plex where seven people escaped injury in July 1982 following a two-alarm fire that occurred in the two-story building. The fire in the 6000 block of Valley Circle began at about 4:00 a.m. Fire officials believe it was started with an "incendiary device" that exploded on a porch south of the building. Below, Lt. Russ Stuve (left) and Battalion Chief Rocky Losli discuss the situation in which tenants escaped by running out of their apartment doors while some jumped from their second-story apartments. A firefighter suffered minor burns during the blaze, which was fought by 25 firefighters. The building was heavily damaged but not so badly that it could not be repaired, fire officials said at the time. (Both photographs by Harvey Thomas, courtesy of TVF&R.)

Yes, those are lions being sprayed by Washington County Fire District No. 1 firefighter Rick Burris on June 12, 1982. The animals, part of Chovani's African Lion Show that was appearing at the Greenway Town Center, were hot from high temperatures during the month, and firefighters agreed to cool them down. The lions "dazzled a few members of the public and many members of the media while cooling off," reported the *Beaverton Valley Times* newspaper, adding that while the cats loved the water, the firefighters were a little apprehensive about spraying the animals. The reward for helping keep the cats' body temperatures low was a visit by a 25-pound lion cub, who was given an up-close-and-personal look inside a fire engine by firefighter Tom Duthie. (Both photographs by Harvey Thomas, courtesy of TVF&R.)

Four

West Linn Fire Department

Even before officially annexing into Tualatin Valley Fire & Rescue in 2004, the West Linn Fire Department had a long, distinguished reputation in the firefighting business.

The department, which included five hose companies, was in full force in 1915. Those hose companies were spread throughout the city with Company No. 1 located at West Linn City Hall, Company No. 2 positioned at Bolton, Companies Nos. 3 and 4 setting up shop in the Sunset area, and Company No. 5 located in the Willamette area.

At the time, hoses, hydrant wrenches, and nozzles were all placed aboard hand-drawn carts that were physically pulled to fires, an interesting endeavor considering that the city includes a series of steep hills and inclines. As time went on and automobiles became a more familiar sight, more and more automobile drivers would volunteer their services in hitching up the carts and pulling them to fires.

Meanwhile, the early stations were not built with architectural elegance as a priority; one of the Sunset stations was nothing more than a utility shed built like an icehouse, the walls stuffed with sawdust to keep the fire engines from freezing. Over at the Bolton station, the company's hose cart was essentially a bunker that had been dug into the dirt at Highway 43 and Barclay Street. In the Sunset area, fire equipment was stored at Winkel's Store, the same store that contained a fire bell that tolled for fires and drills.

A 1929 Model AA flatbed truck was purchased in 1932 for $175. It was retrofitted to fight fires, and the old Crown Zellerbach Paper Mill next to the Willamette River donated one of its welding units to help convert the vehicle to a workable engine and a driver to go with it. By 1946, an engine that would carry 200 gallons of water had been purchased for protection in the Willamette area. (In later years, West Linn Station 59 in the Willamette area would become home to TVF&R's Water Rescue Team.)

Firefighting would enter the modern age in 1967 when three American LaFrance engines were purchased and distributed to stations throughout the city.

In 1952, the Rosemont Fire District was founded and operated until 1990 when the city contracted with West Linn. Rosemont would annex into TVF&R in 2001.

Down the hill, the Robinwood Volunteer Fire Department was established in 1960, charged with responding to calls in the historic Robinwood neighborhood until its annexation to the city in 1969. It would join TVF&R in 2004.

In 1999, Oregon City—a city to the east of West Linn—began contracting emergency services from TVF&R. Founded in 1843, the Oregon City Fire Department is believed to be the oldest paid fire department west of the Mississippi River. The four-year contract with Oregon City ended in 2003 when TVF&R opted not to renew it. Oregon City later began contracting with Clackamas County Fire District No. 1, and in 2007 its voters approved permanent annexation into Clackamas Fire District No. 1.

Members of the West Linn Fire Department pose at the Bolton station in front of their 1942 American LaFrance engine around 1945. They include, from left to right, Ernie Latham, Farrell Heater, Gib Woodard, Bill Anderson, Aaron Thompson, Chief Joe Nixon, Howard Smith, Keith Hadley, Howard Ross, and Gar Schwartz. Eventually, the Bolton station would contain an air-raid

siren that called volunteers to fires. A maximum of 20 volunteers were allowed at the stations by the late 1960s. That same decade, eight firefighters resided on West Linn's historic Buck Street, earning them the nickname "the Buck Street Bandits." (Courtesy of TVF&R.)

Above is West Linn Fire Department's new engine, a 1958 Ford destined for the Sunset-area fire station (Company No. 3). The engine appears below preparing for its next response. The original Sunset station was no more than a small shed built like an icehouse with walls filled with sawdust to keep them from freezing. Winkel's Store, a business in the Sunset area of West Linn, had a small room to store hose nozzles and rolls of hose so that firemen could quickly grab them to take to a fire. Also, Winkel's contained a bell mounted above the store. It was rung for both actual fires and drills. (Both, courtesy of TVF&R.)

This is the Rosemont Fire Hall in 1982 before the current pole building. This Chevrolet sedan was usually driven by Chief Russ Castleman or his assistants. In 1990, the Rosemont Fire District, which was founded in 1952, began to contract with West Linn for service. The Rosemont station is now used for storage. (Courtesy of TVF&R.)

Engines parked in the apron of the Sunset Fire Station include a 1967 American LaFrance (left) and a 1958 Ford. The aging Sunset station is still used as a community center. (Courtesy of TVF&R.)

The Robinwood Fire Department, an all-volunteer group, was established in 1960 and annexed into the city of West Linn in 1969. This photograph features a portion of personnel in 1965, including, from left to right, Chief Bill Bryant, Capt. Ray Gibbens, and firefighters Joe Hamel and Claude Hampton. (Courtesy of TVF&R.)

West Linn firefighters practice drills with some of their equipment, including a 1967 American LaFrance engine (center) and the department's 1958 Ford (left). The vehicle sticking out at right is believed to be a 1946 pumper that carried 200 gallons of water and was used to protect the Willamette area. (Courtesy of TVF&R.)

West Linn Fire Department firefighters from Engine Company No. 2 appear around 1945. In 1932, the department purchased a 1929 Model AA flatbed truck for $175, converting it for use as an engine. In 1946, a pumper that could carry 200 gallons of water was purchased to serve the Willamette area. Later, West Linn would make a large step forward, purchasing three American LaFrance engines and retiring the Model AA in 1967. (Courtesy of TVF&R.)

West Linn firefighters practice with their 1967 American LaFrance engine. This was one of three purchased from the manufacturer, which was then located in Elmira, New York. Chief Joe Nixon and another firefighter took delivery of one of the engines for the Bolton Fire Station at the time, but a rollover accident on their way home would result in a year delay before the engine made it back into service in West Linn. The other two engines ended up in the Sunset and Willamette stations. (Courtesy of TVF&R.)

Firefighters from the West Linn Fire Department's Bolton station pose in front of Engine No. 2, a 1942 American LaFrance (left), and the 1929 Model AA flatbed truck. Chief Joe Nixon is fourth from the left. Nixon joined the department in 1923 and remained a volunteer until his death in 1976. (Courtesy of TVF&R.)

West Linn firefighters practice a drill using one of three 1967 engines purchased from the American LaFrance company, one of the oldest fire equipment manufacturers in the nation. (Courtesy of TVF&R.)

Firefighters from the West Linn Fire Department battle the Willamette Grade School fire in 1989. The fire was fought for two days with help from the department's TELESQURT. Among those who battled the blaze were firefighters Bob Tice and Richard Block. It was not the first time a school bearing the same name caught fire. On January 5, 1949, the second Willamette Grade School, which was built under a Federal Grant Project, burned down. (Courtesy of TVF&R.)

Glen "Windy" Wenzinger and Sparky the firedog ride in a parade in the 1990s aboard the 1929 Model AA (it had dual rear tires, hence the AA designation) that he spent two years refurbishing. After having the engine sandblasted and repainted, Wenzinger added a 13-foot oak running board. On a January 8, 1983, trip to downtown Portland to have the vehicle further restored, Wenzinger and fellow firefighter Harland Geigle saw a pickup truck on fire. Grabbing the 40-pound carbon dioxide portable extinguisher mounted on the side of the vehicle, the pair put out the fire even before the Portland Fire Bureau arrived with an aerial truck. For their efforts, they received letters of thanks from both West Linn and Portland officials. (Both, courtesy Oregon City Fire Department.)

Here is an early engine parked in front of Oregon City's main station in the 1920s. The Oregon City Fire Department is believed to be the oldest paid fire department west of the Mississippi River, founded in 1843. Its first station was located at the base of the historic Willamette Falls. Early hose cart companies all had distinctive names. For example, Hose Company No. 3 was known as the Soda Hose Company because they "took no libations." Tualatin Valley Fire & Rescue provided fire protection and emergency medical services for Oregon City for about four years. Oregon City later signed a contract with Clackamas County Fire District No. 1 to provide services and later annexed to Clackamas County Fire District No. 1. (Both, courtesy Oregon City Fire Department.)

While it is not immediately clear which stations are shown here, Oregon City's oldest station, Station 54, was built in 1925 at Seventh and John Adams Streets in a historic part of the city. A home down the street once belonged to Dr. John McLoughlin, chief factor of the Hudson's Bay Company, who laid claim to land from Willamette Falls to the Clackamas River. Tualatin Valley Fire & Rescue provided service to Oregon City on a contract basis from 1999 to 2003. (Both, courtesy of TVF&R.)

Five

Behind the Scenes

Although it happened more than three decades ago, firefighter Terry Bowman can vividly remember that warm spring day that would change his life: March 19, 1979, the day the Beaverton High School auditorium caught fire, quickly escalating into a four-alarm blaze.

Because of the warm weather, Bowman, then a 36-year-old firefighter with Washington County Fire District No. 1, had only his turnout pants on but not the jacket. He went on the roof via an aerial ladder to hand off a chainsaw to his fellow firefighters when the roof became soft; he knew it would not hold much longer. As he jumped onto a nearby aerial ladder, the auditorium roof collapsed, sending flames shooting skyward and engulfing Bowman in the process.

On the ground, fellow firefighters doused the flames. Bowman's shirt had melted on his body. He suffered second- and third-degree burns over 49 percent of his body—the worst burns suffered by a TVF&R firefighter.

"I just wasn't supposed to be up there, but you know, firefighters get excited," he said. "I was burned from the waist up."

The heat also melted both his eye glasses and helmet.

Since that day, fire departments throughout the country have used a television crew's video of Bowman coming down the ladder on fire to stress the importance of wearing protective clothing.

After recovering for six months, Bowman returned to his job and did not retire until more than a decade later. So why did he go back to an occupation that so drastically changed his life? "It's the best job there is," he said.

Since that 1979 fire, there have been other major fires throughout the fire district. However, the worst was on June 26, 1996, when a fire at the Oakwood Park Apartments in Aloha killed eight people. An 11-year-old boy was subsequently charged and convicted of starting the fire.

That tragedy resulted in the district beginning the Apartment Fire Incident and Education Program (AFIRE) program, which included weekend safety events at apartment complexes deemed as high risk for fires along with the implementation of a bilingual educational program about fire safety.

Despite being an often-dangerous profession, firefighting also has its offbeat incidents and lighter, behind-the-scenes moments, one of which came when the district's Technical Rescue Team helped retrieve a tranquilized bear from a tree.

TVF&R firefighters also participate in the annual Scott Firefighter Stairclimb, the largest firefighter competition in the world, held each year in Seattle. They have also been past participants in the West Coast Giant Pumpkin Regatta where participants navigate around a lake in downtown Tualatin in 1,000-pound, carved-out pumpkins.

Mike Duyck was appointed fire chief of TVF&R in 2010. He began his career in the fire service in 1988 as a firefighter with the Lake Oswego Fire Department. In 1989, while still a firefighter with Lake Oswego, he worked part-time in TVF&R's Fleet Services. In 1995, he became a full-time firefighter with TVF&R. His career with the district includes all ranks within emergency services, as well as fleet services, human resources, logistics, and government affairs. (Courtesy of TVF&R.)

Jeff Johnson served as fire chief of Tualatin Valley Fire & Rescue for 15 years, retiring in 2010. He joined the fire district in 1989 following an 11-year fire service career in Douglas County. He is a past president of the International Association of Fire Chiefs. (Courtesy of TVF&R.)

Former chief Jack Snook became the first chief of the merged Tualatin Valley Fire & Rescue in 1989. Snook previously served as chief of the Lake Oswego Fire Department and was named chief of Washington County Fire District No. 1 in 1986. After receiving a heart transplant while serving as TVF&R chief, Snook resumed his duties 67 days later. He retired in 1994 but is still active in business endeavors related to fire services. (Courtesy of Jack Snook.)

Marilyn Kosel became the first female firefighter to join the Beaverton Fire Department in 1986. She later worked out of Cedar Mill Station No. 255 after the formation of Tualatin Valley Fire & Rescue. Today, the district has numerous women working in a variety of positions throughout the district. (Photograph by Vern Uyetake, courtesy of Community Newspapers.)

Here are firefighter and emergency medical services patches and badges collected by Frank Oulman, a Beaverton Fire Department employee from 1973 to 1996. In 1978, the Beaverton Fire Department saw a need for coordinating medical services and hired Oulman as its first emergency medical services coordinator. (Courtesy of Frank Oulman.)

In addition to being a firefighter/paramedic, Russ Williamson also was a member of the Scappoose Fire District's board of directors. He is believed to have been the only firefighter killed while on duty in recent history, struck by a truck while outside a fire station. Before joining Washington County Fire District No. 1, Williamson was a volunteer at the St. Helen's Fire Department. (Courtesy of TVF&R.)

Firefighters (including, Dwight Douglas, Washington County Fire District No. 1's first chaplain, at left) stand at attention as a memorial bell is dedicated on May 29, 1984, in honor of firefighter Russ Williamson. At age 28, Williamson was struck by a truck while he played his guitar outside the former Aloha Fire Station on 185th Avenue on May 8, 1978. He died several days later. The memorial is located in the front of what was then administrative headquarters for Washington County Fire District No. 1 on Blanton Street. In front of the memorial bell, Dan Atkinson pays his respects. Firefighter Williamson worked for WCFD No. 1 for five years, four of them as a paramedic on Rescue Team 5. (Both photographs by Harvey Thomas, courtesy of TVF&R.)

Above, Oscar "Sox" Lee (left), Beaverton Fire Department chief from 1985 to 1991, receives congratulations from Beaverton mayor Larry Cole during Lee's retirement party in 1991. Earlier in his career, Lee worked for the state fire marshal's office and previously worked at area community colleges teaching fire science classes. He came to Beaverton as a training officer in 1970, a job he enjoyed immensely. Lee was among the Beaverton firefighters who responded to the Beaverton High School fire in 1979 where firefighter Terry Bowman was severely burned after a roof collapsed. "That was one of the worst days of my life when Terry was burned," he said. (Both, courtesy of Oscar "Sox" Lee.)

The Oscar Mayer Wienermobile is washed with the help of SQURT 62 behind the Aloha Station located on 209th Avenue. Constructed in 1980, the station replaced an aging facility on 185th Avenue. Washing the Wienermobile, even with a high-pressure hose, is no easy feat, as the vehicle is 27 feet long and 11 feet tall. (Courtesy of TVF&R.)

Lt. Al Edens (left), an unidentified firefighter (center), and Art Thurber ventilate the roof of the Beaverton High School theater shortly before it collapsed. Retired firefighter Capt. Ernie Metcalfe climbed up to shoot this photograph before climbing down to get more air bottles. Moments later, "the whole damn thing blew and got Terry," recalled Metcalfe. Terry Bowman was engulfed in flames as soon as he stepped on an aerial ladder. (Photograph by Ernie Metcalfe.)

Truck 252 shoots "master streams" in an effort to extinguish the Beaverton High School theater fire of 1979. When firefighter Terry Bowman caught fire, he tried to get down the aerial ladder as fast as he could. However, by the time he reached the ground, he had serious burns over 49 percent of his body, the worst ever suffered by a TVF&R firefighter as far back as anyone can remember. (Photograph by Ernie Metcalfe.)

Here is a view of the devastation inside the Beaverton High School theater after the March 19, 1979, fire. The four-alarm blaze required 15 pieces of apparatus to control the fire, including nine engines, three trucks, and four rescue units. (David Nieslanik collection, courtesy of the Beaverton Historical Society.)

Terry Bowman displays the helmet that melted during the Beaverton High School fire of 1979. Although badly burned (it took six months before he was back at work, and he had to wear special clothes for his burns during the next two years), he worked for the fire district until the early 1990s. Today, Bowman lives on the Oregon Coast and is still involved with the fire services. (Photograph by Vern Uyetake, courtesy of Community Newspapers.)

June 1, 2011, was not a typical day for firefighters, who joined police and emergency personnel in pursuing this 200-pound black bear (above) that was running loose near Tualatin Elementary School and a nearby housing development. Students watched from inside their school as the bear eventually climbed up a tree and was tranquilized by two darts. Both Oregon Fish and Wildlife and Tualatin Valley Fire & Rescue crews worked for three hours to fasten a rope around the animal to safely bring him down. TVF&R Technical Rescue Team member Don Schulte (center) helped remove a makeshift harness once the animal was on the ground. (Above, photograph by Jaime Valdez, courtesy of Community Newspapers; below, courtesy of TVF&R.)

An old oak tree decided to "give up and fall over" in October 1994, according to retired Washington County Fire District No. 1 firefighter Steve May. This was not such an unusual event, except that there was no wind that day and the tree fell on the vehicles of two firefighters who were at the old Jenkins Road station celebrating the retirement of another firefighter. (Photograph by Steve May.)

Pictured from left to right, alarm operator Mel Watt, John Robinson, Washington County Fire District No. 1 chief Walt Platt, and Cedar Mill fire marshal Hubert May all gather during a retiree award ceremony. (Courtesy of TVF&R.)

The Willamette Industries fire at 5500 Southwest Western Avenue in Beaverton on February 20, 1990, gutted the warehouse in what is still one of the largest commercial fires in district memory. More than 100 firefighters responded to the warehouse, which was used to store cardboard and paper products. The six-alarm blaze, which left only the four exterior walls intact, resulted in injuries to four firefighters, including Tualatin Valley Fire & Rescue chief Jack Snook along with Mike Hart, John Schwartz, and Bert Parker during mop-up operations. Both Snook and Hart were knocked unconscious by a plywood section, which weighed between 400 and 500 pounds. All were treated and released. The cause of the blaze was dust that had collected above the rafters and on top of sprinkler heads that in turn was ignited by a space heater. (Left, courtesy of Community Newspapers; below, photograph by Vern Uyetake, courtesy of Community Newspapers.)

Washington County Fire District No. 1 firefighter Bob Armstrong (in sunglasses) helps firefighter Jim Murfitt operate a nozzle during an Albany fire muster, a timed competition involving antique fire equipment in 1982. The competitive pair racked up numerous ribbons at various musters. (Photograph by Steve May.)

Three months after the Willamette Industries fire—one of the largest commercial fires in TVF&R history—a second fire hit a commercial warehouse. On May 18, 1990, Stanton Industries, a furniture warehouse in Tualatin, was gutted by a four-alarm fire that caused millions of dollars in damage. Although the 40,000-square-foot building was equipped with sprinklers, the fire overran them. Smoker carelessness was listed as the cause of the fire. (Photograph by Vern Uyetake, courtesy of Community Newspapers.)

Rudy Oliveros strums a guitar in the Sherwood Station where he worked as a fireman for 12 years as a Tualatin Valley Fire & Rescue employee. Prior to that, Oliveros was at Beaverton's Brockman Road station where he had the distinction of being the first Hispanic hired by the Beaverton Fire Department. After 36 years with TVF&R, Oliveros retired in July 2011. (Courtesy of TVF&R.)

Washington Fire District No. 1 chief Walt Platt (left) Ben Kincaid, and Greg Henrick (right) check to see if Wayne Wright's (in helmet) hair meets grooming standards. In 1972, Platt became the district's first chief, having previously served as chief of the Beaverton Rural Fire Protection District. (Courtesy of TVF&R.)

It was not only hard work fighting fires. There was time for some fun as well. Here, Howard Ross (left), Ernie Wallace (center), and Howard Smith take a break after competition in the 1948 Clackamas County Fair hose coupling contest. They won with a time of 3 minutes, 22 seconds. (Photograph from West Linn Fire Department, courtesy of TVF&R.)

During the January 18, 1974, flood, firefighter Jim McGuire measures water in the Tualatin Rural Fire Protection District's main station, located then at Southwest Eighty-fourth Avenue and Seneca Street. The water went as high as three feet on some parts of Boones Ferry Road, according to one retired fire official. (Courtesy of Sherwood Volunteer Firefighters' Association.)

Arcing wires from a fire at the Terrace Apartments in the 1960s kept West Slope Fire District firefighters busy. The 3:25 a.m. fire was blamed on an electric bulb used to heat a cardboard doghouse. The dog survived, but the dog of another apartment resident was not so lucky. The fire virtually destroyed one apartment and caused extensive smoke, water, and fire damage to another. (Courtesy of TVF&R.)

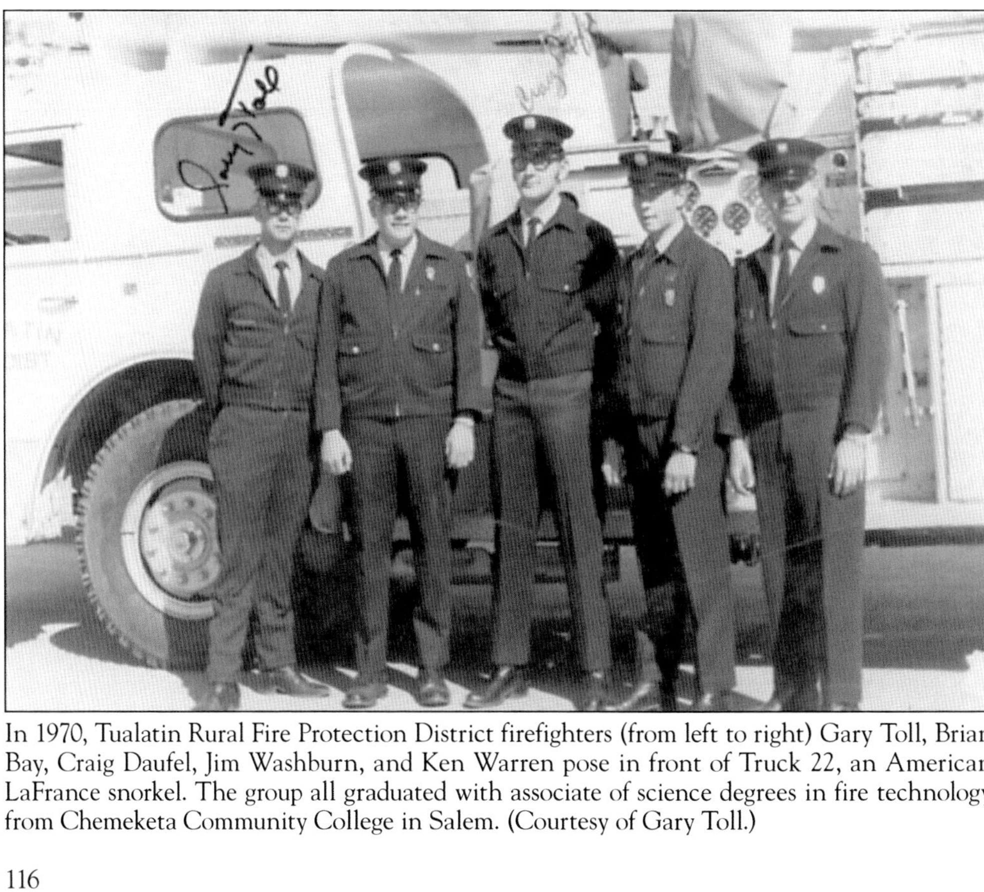

In 1970, Tualatin Rural Fire Protection District firefighters (from left to right) Gary Toll, Brian Bay, Craig Daufel, Jim Washburn, and Ken Warren pose in front of Truck 22, an American LaFrance snorkel. The group all graduated with associate of science degrees in fire technology from Chemeketa Community College in Salem. (Courtesy of Gary Toll.)

Washington County Fire District No. 1 firefighters (from left to right) Bob Tappert, Greg Henrick, and Dave Herndon peel back a tin roof as they battle a May 17, 1977, fire on Helvetia Road, north of Highway 26. The fire was actually in Washington County Fire District No. 2's jurisdiction, but District No. 1 responded as part of a mutual aid agreement, according to Harvey Thomas, a longtime photographer for WCFD No. 1. The fire was believed to have started in the home's kitchen. Newspapers stacked to the ceiling in almost every room fueled the blaze, he said. Also, 12-inch-thick plaster ceilings on the second floor hampered firefighters. However, once they were able to pull the tin off the roof, as seen in this photograph, they were able to extinguish the fire. The homeowner went on to repair the damage and moved back in, recalled Thomas. (Photograph by Harvey Thomas.)

In 1989, Oregon became the first state in the nation to create a statewide Regional Hazardous Materials Emergency Response system. TVF&R's team, comprised of 30 highly trained responders, is one of only 14 teams in Oregon that responds to fires, spills, and other incidents involving chemicals and toxic materials. (Courtesy of TVF&R.)

In 2006, voters in TVF&R's district approved a $77.5-million bond measure to rebuild and upgrade fire stations and purchase emergency response apparatus. Building a new fire station to serve the Greater Tigard/Beaverton area was one of the projects. The station, located on Walnut Street in Tigard, was the district's first new station to be added in 10 years and its first LEED-certified station. The Leadership in Energy and Environmental Design (LEED) designation verifies that the station is recognized as a "green" building. (Courtesy of TVF&R.)

A demonstration at Tualatin Valley Fire & Rescue's Training Center in the summer of 2011 showed just how fast and effective a home sprinkling system can douse fires. Firefighters at the facility set up side-by-side mock-ups of typical living rooms. The fire on the unsprinkled (right side) of the demonstration facility quickly escalated, flashing over before firefighters extinguished it. However, the fire in the living room with sprinklers (left side) was quickly extinguished before it had time to build. (Photograph by author, courtesy of Community Newspapers.)

Here is what firefighters at the West Slope station looked like in the early 2000s, a marked difference from the 1960s when turnouts were no more than rubber-lined coats with canvas coverings. The West Slope Station at 8661 Southwest Canyon Road, which also serves residents in Raleigh Hills, is expected to be replaced soon, as of this October 2011 writing. (Courtesy of TVF&R.)

In 2003, Tualatin Valley Fire & Rescue implemented a daylong training program for apartment landlords. The training is designed to help landlords create safer apartment communities and includes an opportunity to use a fire extinguisher. In 2006, the program received one of the nation's most prestigious awards: the International Association of Fire Chiefs' Fire Service Award for Excellence. (Courtesy of TVF&R.)

Dick Morgan (left), of Washington County Fire District No. 1, helps a fellow firefighter get some oxygen in the mid-1970s. In 1967, a decade earlier, 50 District No. 1 firefighters ended up in the emergency room at St. Vincent Hospital in Northwest Portland following a four-alarm fire that began at Tektronix's Beaverton campus. It was later determined that many of the firefighters had possibly been exposed to several different chemicals. All were released after 24 hours of observation. (Courtesy of TVF&R.)

Jerry Heater uses his emergency radio to communicate during the May 1971 Conrad Smeltzer house fire in Sherwood. "He knew everything about fire service apparatus," said Don Anderson, a retired Tualatin Rural Fire Protection District community information officer. "He was really well thought of." (Courtesy of Sherwood Volunteer Firefighters' Association.)

The day the two new Pirsch engines arrived in Beavertown in June 1962, a spontaneous celebration broke out aboard the 1935 engine shown parked here at Luther's Grocery Store at 114th Avenue and Canyon Road. The older vehicle was discovered to have a frozen pump during a "burn to learn" exercise, so the other vehicles could not arrive soon enough. Jo Winters (left) joined with Perry and Mrs. Weinberger and numerous unidentified children. Beaverton firefighter Joe Thomas is at the far right. (Photograph by Ernie Metcalfe.)

Firefighters from the Tualatin Rural Fire Protection District pose after a controlled house burn on Fischer Road just off Highway 99 around 1971. They include, from left to right, (first row) Lt. Guy Scull, firefighter Kevin Munson, firefighter Craig Dauffle, engineer Buzz Williams, student firefighter Grant Williams, and student firefighter Jim Chambers; (second row) firefighter Tony Tucker, Lt. Eldon Johnson, Lt. Bill Gilliam, Greg Fall, and unidentified. (Courtesy of Jim Chambers.)

J.E. Morback, once the mayor of Sherwood, stands proudly in front of the handmade fire engine built by him and the town's police chief, whose last name was Zimmerman. Although it looks like a factory-manufactured engine, it did not go very fast (perhaps 10 to 15 miles per hour), according to Sherwood historian Clyde List. The Morback House, which now houses the Sherwood Historical Society, is in the background. (Courtesy of Clyde List.)

Just how messy a job firefighting can be is seen on the turnouts and face of West Slope fire chief Hueston Reynolds during a May 1962 house fire on Southwest Florence Lane in the West Slope area. Firefighters from the Beaverton Rural Fire Protection District also helped out with this fire. Reynolds, a former Lake Grove fire chief, was hired as chief in 1960, resigning in 1963 to take the helm of the Beaverton Fire Department. (Courtesy of TVF&R.)

Firefighters train at TVF&R's Regional Training Center in Sherwood. Built in 1992, the center features modern classrooms and training props, allowing firefighters to train in technical rescue, hazardous materials, and water rescue scenarios. Situated on 15.65 acres, the center contains propane burn props along with confined-space, trench, and high-angle rescue scenarios and scenes along with a HazMat response area. (Courtesy of TVF&R.)

Tualatin Valley Fire & Rescue firefighters battle a three-acre hay-field fire in July 2010 on Southwest Lebeau Road in a rural area south of Sherwood. (The hay had been scheduled to be baled the next day.) The two-alarm fire was hampered by temperatures in the mid-90s and strong south winds. (Photograph by Jaime Valdez, courtesy of Community Newspapers.)

This 1976 Seagrave pumper was one of two purchased by Washington County Fire District No. 1, later serving at the Progress and Aloha stations. When TVF&R consolidated, it became a volunteer apparatus stationed in Tigard before it was retired in 1999. Volunteer firefighter Jeff Butts purchased it in 2001 and spent about six months bringing it to its original grandeur. In 2010, he "gifted" it to the Mist-Birkenfeld Rural Fire Protection District. (Photograph courtesy of Jeff Butts.)

Beaverton police and Tualatin Valley Fire & Rescue firefighters pay respects to all of the first responders who lost their lives trying to rescue others from the World Trade Center on September 11, 2001, at the 10-year commemorative flag ceremony that was held at the downtown Beaverton Fire Station in September 2011. Tim Birr (right), a longtime member and founder of TVF&R's Pipes and Drums, plays bagpipes during the solemn event. (Photograph by Jaime Valdez, courtesy of Community Newspapers.)

Tualatin Valley Fire & Rescue firefighter Tim Buchanon shakes the hand of four-year-old Christian Tofte and his dad, Paul, during a tour of the Tigard station following a candlelight vigil held on September 15, 2001. The vigil was in response to the September 11, 2001, terrorist attacks. (Photograph by Jaime Valdez, courtesy of Community Newspapers.)

An unidentified Tualatin Valley Fire & Rescue firefighter shares a quiet moment during a flag march and candlelight vigil in downtown Tigard held four days after the September 11, 2001, terrorist attacks. More than 500 people joined police, firefighters, and city hall employees during the Main Street march where they sang patriotic songs and paid tribute to all of those who lost their lives. (Photograph by Jaime Valdez, courtesy of Community Newspapers.)

Bibliography

Anderson, Don. "Fifty Years of Service 1935–1985: Tualatin Fire District." Written history from Tualatin Valley Fire & Rescue internal archives, 1985.

Beaverton: 75 Years of Progress Diamond Jubilee Issue 1893–1968. Beaverton, OR: *Beaverton Valley Times*, 1968.

"Beaverton Rural Fire Protection District." Written history from Tualatin Valley Fire & Rescue internal archives, 2002.

Bruton, Lynn, Scott Sullivan, and Kurt Koudelka. *Tualatin Valley Fire & Rescue*. Minneapolis, MN: Jostens, 2002.

Coleman, Lee. Interview by Ray Pitz, August 2011.

Coleman, Lee. "West Slope: History of the Department." Written history from Tualatin Valley Fire & Rescue internal archives, 2002.

Johnson, Jeff. Interview by Ray Pitz, August 2011.

Mapes, Virginia. *Chakeipi: The Place of the Beaver*. Tigard, OR: Community Newspapers, 1993.

Martin, Joe. "Sherwood, Oregon Fire Department." Written history from Tualatin Valley Fire & Rescue internal archives, 2006.

Lee, Oscar "Sox." Interview by Ray Pitz, August 2011.

Metcalfe, Ernie. Interview by Ray Pitz, August and September 2011.

Metcalfe, Ernie, and Jim St. Claire. "Beaverton Fire Department." Written history from Tualatin Valley Fire & Rescue internal archives, 2002.

Oulman, Frank. "Beaverton EMS History." Written history from Tualatin Valley Fire & Rescue internal archives, 2011.

Reynolds, June. *Sherwood: A Sense of Time and Place*. Vol. 1, *Beginnings to 1919*. Sherwood, OR: Cheyenne Printing, 2006.

Snook, Jack. Interview by Ray Pitz, August 2011.

"Washington County Fire District No. 1." Written history from Tualatin Valley Fire & Rescue internal archives, 2002.

Wenzinger, Glen "Windy." Interview by Ray Pitz, August 2011.

"West Linn Fire Department." Written history from Tualatin Valley Fire & Rescue internal archives, 2002.